THE ESSENCE OF

DISTRIBUTED SYSTEMS

THE ESSENCE OF COMPUTING SERIES

THE ESSENCE OF

DISTRIBUTED SYSTEMS

Joel M. Crichlow

Prentice
Hall

An imprint of **Pearson Education**
Harlow, England · London · New York · Reading, Massachusetts · San Francisco · Toronto · Don Mills, Ontario · Sydney
Tokyo · Singapore · Hong Kong · Seoul · Taipei · Cape Town · Madrid · Mexico City · Amsterdam · Munich · Paris · Milan

Pearson Education Limited
Edinburgh Gate
Harlow, Essex CM20 2JE
England

and Associated Companies around the World.

Visit us on the World Wide Web at:
www.pearsoneduc.com

First published 2000

© Pearson Education Limited 2000

ISBN 0130-15167-X

British Library Cataloguing-in-Publication Data
A catalogue record for this book can be obtained from the British Library

Library of Congress Cataloging-in-Publication Data
Crichlow, Joel M., 1948-
    The essence of distributed systems / Joel M. Crichlow.
        p.   cm. -- (Essence of computing series)
    Includes bibliographical references.
    ISBN 0-13-015167-X
    1. Electronic data processing--Distributed processing.   I. Title.
    II. Series.
    QA76.9.D5C747   1999
    004'.36--dc21   99-41802
                                                             CIP

10 9 8 7 6 5 4 3 2 1
04 03 02 01 00

Typeset by 43 in 10pt Times
Printed in Great Britain by Henry Ling Ltd., at the Dorset Press, Dorchester, Dorset

Contents

Series Preface

As the consulting editor for the Essence of Computing Series it is my role to encourage the production of well-focused, high-quality textbooks at prices which students can afford. Since most computing courses are modular in structure, we aim to produce books which will cover the essential material for a typical module.

I want to maintain a consistent style for the Series so that whenever you pick up an Essence book you know what to expect. For example, each book contains important features such as end of chapter summaries and exercises, and a glossary of terms, if appropriate. Of course, the quality of the Series depends crucially on the skills of its authors and all the books are written by lecturers who have honed their material in the classroom. Each book in the Series takes a pragmatic approach and emphasises practical examples and case studies.

Our aim is that each book will become essential reading material for students attending core modules in Computing. However, we expect students to want to go beyond the Essence books and so all books contain guidance on further reading and related work.

Distributed systems are now in widespread use throughout a wide range of computing application areas and an understanding of their fundamental principles is an essential part of the computing curriculum. There are many technical challenges that come from moving away from a single stand-alone computer system to a complex network of heterogeneous machines. The core of this book is a systematic presentation of the basic issues in building distributed systems, particularly different architectures and resource issues. It includes material about different applications of distributed systems and case studies to illustrate the important issues. The other feature of this book is that it draws upon material from a number of parts of the computing curriculum, such as computer systems, operating systems, programming and databases; bridging a number of disparate areas.

Computing is constantly evolving and so the teaching of the subject also has to change. Therefore, the Series has to be dynamic, responding to new trends in computing and extending into new areas of interest. We need feedback from our readers to guide us – are we hitting the target? Are there 'hot' topics which we have not covered yet? Feedback is always welcome but most of all I hope you find this book useful!

Ray Welland
Department of Computing Science
University of Glasgow
(e-mail: ray@dcs.gla.ac.uk)

Preface

Distributed systems operate on computer network platforms. However, a primary objective is to make the user feel that he or she is working on a single computer. Furthermore, as the user moves from one computer to another, he or she should find no significant change in the interface to the system. This text deals with the key issues pertinent to the design and construction of a distributed system. The design and construction of distributed systems are highly technical and very time-consuming endeavours, which usually require the involvement of skilled project teams. After studying this text you should be able to participate effectively in such a project team.

Some pre-requisite knowledge in Computer Science is necessary. Specifically, you should have completed courses in computer programming, computer organization, data structures, file design, fundamentals of operating systems and database design. If you do not have this background, you may still find much of the material not too difficult to follow.

The text follows mainly (in rather general terms) a top-down or outside to inside approach. There are seven chapters. Chapter 1 is an introduction which sets distributed systems within the context of present computer technology, highlights some of the key service areas and presents the significant design concerns. Chapter 2 looks at major distributed system applications. Chapter 3 examines distributed system architectures.

In Chapters 4 to 6 we address the issues pertaining to the handling and accessing of resources in the distributed system. The resources can be data, programs, hardware units, etc. The issues can be classified as general (e.g. naming, addressing) as opposed to the more special purpose (e.g. distributed shared memory). Chapters 4 and 5 deal with the general, while Chapter 6 deals with the special.

Categorizing and ordering the general issues are not straightforward tasks. Two complementary (and sometimes intersecting) perspectives have been adopted. On the one hand the resources are looked at from the point of view of the manager (or store-keeper), and on the other hand from the perspective of those accessing the resource. Chapter 4 concentrates on the management matters and Chapter 5 highlights the accessing problems. In Chapter 7 the focus is on case studies.

Thanks are due to the editorial staff and reviewers of Prentice Hall Europe and Pearson Education for their expert guidance during the preparation of this text. I also thank my colleagues at U.W.I. for their support, and I am indebted to my wife Valerie and my children for their invaluable encouragement. Thanks to God in whom 'we live, and move, and have our being'.

J.M.C.
St Augustine
joel@centre.uwi.tt
essence_of_ds@hotmail.com
1999

CHAPTER 1

Introduction

We yearn to be well informed, to keep up-to-date, to communicate. The ubiquitous presence of the print media, the electronic media and the tele-communications infrastructure is the result of this yearning. The computer is now well embedded in the information-sharing structure. The computer storage, processing and retrieval capabilities are the primary reasons for the computer's key role in our present-day information-sharing and retrieval culture. Equally significant is the role that telecommunication is playing in providing global sharing of computational resources – software and hardware.

The Internet and the World Wide Web have virtually removed the cap on what information can be obtained, from whom or where, and at what time. We can, via remote job entry systems, log on and run computer programs on computers vast distances away; and with software like Java we can import programs from remote Web sites and execute them in real time on our local computer.

The *distributed system* is set against this background. A distributed system is a set of interconnected, autonomous computers that cooperatively solve large, single problems or facilitate parallel execution of separate, but possibly related tasks (Wittie, 1991). Furthermore, the distributed system should appear to the user as a single computer, and the user's interface with the system should remain the same, in its significant aspects, irrespective of which computer that user is working on.

Three key attributes can be highlighted from this definition. Firstly, there is a network of computers facilitating on-line computer to computer communication and the sharing of processing functions. Secondly, the network is hidden from the user; and thirdly, the system looks the same wherever the user is working (see Figure 1.1).

The sharing of the processing functions among computers is a significant distinguishing feature between a distributed system and other networked systems. There are many on-line time-sharing systems which, via a communications network, allow users concurrent access to a centralized, computerized resource. As long as all the processing is in one place and, therefore, no need exists for multi-computer coordination, the system cannot be called 'distributed'.

A system which allows remote login to run programs on a supercomputer is therefore not a distributed system. A system which allows remote searching of a

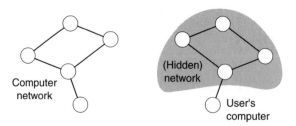

Figure 1.1 The user views the distributed system as a single computer.

centralized database is also not distributed. However, an airline reservations system which maintains multiple copies of its database in a mutually consistent state, and which allows concurrent access by transactions to these copies, is a distributed system.

Even as we attempt to make this distinction between distributed systems and what may be considered as merely networked systems, we hasten to indicate that there is enough cloudiness around the boundaries to fuel a lot of controversy among both the theorists and the practitioners. However, what is clear is that in a distributed system there exist a computer network, task sharing, coordination and some autonomy (see Coulouris *et al.*, 1994; Crichlow, 1997; Tanenbaum, 1995).

1.1 The computer network

A computer network includes the computers on which the users run their programs or applications and a communications subnet. The users' computers are called hosts, stations or autonomous computers. The communication subnet is an interconnection of communication processors.

This communication subnet is the environment where the main communication functions are undertaken. The communication processor is usually referred to as an **IMP (Interface Message Processor)** or a **PSN (Packet Switching Node)** (see Figure 1.2). These PSNs, depending on their specific function, have been variously and sometimes loosely classified in the industry as switches, hubs, bridges, gateways and routers.

Networks are usually grouped into three broad classes: the wide area network (**WAN**), the local area network (**LAN**) and the metropolitan area network (**MAN**). The WAN covers a wide geographic area, even connecting continents, whereas the LAN covers a small area, e.g. an office block, a university campus or even a single room. The MAN is essentially an intra-city link.

Computer network development has benefited significantly from the pioneering work done by **ARPA** (Advanced Research Projects Agency) of the US Department of Defense (now called DARPA). They gave us **ARPANET** in the late 1960s, on which many fundamental issues have been tried and tested, from where

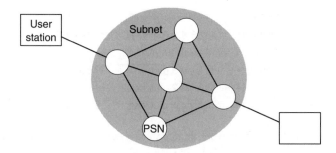

Figure 1.2 Computer network includes hosts and a communications subnet of PSNs.

many network terms have originated, and from which came the principal foundational contributions to our present-day Internet, which links millions of computers around the world.

Designers must address several communication issues. These include:

(a) the quantity and quality of information that the communication link can carry;
(b) the choice of a suitable communication medium;
(c) the sharing of the communication channel among the many users; and
(d) the development and maintenance of an acceptable level of reliability in the transfer of information.

Modularity in design has always been recommended as a sensible approach to systems design. This is necessary, especially in the design of large software systems. Modularity allows the global task to be divided into manageable subtasks, thus facilitating concentrated effort by smaller specialist project teams. Easier maintenance, efficient upgrade and expansion also follow from modularity.

Computer networks have been built along modular lines. The architecture involves a number of layers, each layer being implemented at all the hosts. The layers must range from the hardware or physical level to the user level. Each layer will then behave as if it is communicating only with the corresponding layer at the other sites. Guidelines must be established to permit this layer-to-layer communication. Such guidelines are usually referred to as **protocols**.

Therefore the situation that obtains between two hosts can be expressed as in Figure 1.3. The actual transfer of information occurs only at the lowest layer, i.e. the physical layer.

In addition to matters of architecture, there are also matters of topology. This covers issues concerning where to locate the computers and how to link them together so as to minimize cost and at the same time achieve acceptable levels of performance.

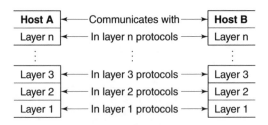

Figure 1.3 Layered network architecture. Each layer communicates with its peer layer.

1.2 Services

Several of the applications that run on a network platform, as has been indicated above, cannot be classified as distributed systems. However, arguably all the services available via networked applications can be provided by distributed systems. We will look at some of these services. In so doing we will make reference to several product, system and protocol names. To those that are key to distributed systems we shall return later in the text. However, the references at the end of the book provide additional reading on all the services.

1.2.1 Electronic mail

The electronic mail service, commonly referred to as *email*, has established itself as the first choice for peer-to-peer communication in many areas of our daily activities. Email allows one to send messages of widely varying length, ranging from the insignificant to the top-security type to registered users on the network or interconnected networks.

The email service is obtained either by keying in the appropriate 'mail' command or clicking on a 'mail' icon. The primary functions provided are 'send mail' and 'read mail'. However, all email systems provide many useful additional functions.

The mail system is usually structured as two primary interacting modules. One module interacts with the user. It facilitates the writing and reading of mail and many other messaging functions. This module may be called the user agent or mail reader, or sometimes just the mail program. The other module interacts with the communication network. It handles the transfer of mail from computer to computer and is often called the message transfer agent.

Some examples of widely used mail readers are Eudora, Hotmail, Pegasus, Pine, Outlook and Yahoo. In addition to sending and reading mail, these programs let you save or delete mail, reply to mail and forward mail to other addresses, and have other useful features. Furthermore, there is access to Internet news and support for **MIME** (Multipurpose Internet Mail Extensions).

With MIME one is not restricted to text messages coded in ASCII. MIME accommodates a comprehensive range of types in the mail documents. Some example types are richtext, postscript, image, audio and video, each of which forms an integral part of our multimedia world. Richtext allows document preparation indicators (indentation, bold, italics, etc.) to be transmitted with the message. This is done by employing a standardized markup language. Postscript documents are received in their final printed-page format. The image type affords the transmission of still pictures. Audio and video, as the names imply, are for sound and moving pictures respectively.

The message transfer agent will put the sending message on and take the receiving mail off the network. In order to do this the agent must follow some established protocol or protocols. Indeed, if one wants to communicate with someone, whether face-to-face or via computers over a network, one must follow the rules. For example, one must first get the other party's attention.

The protocols which govern the interactions over a computer network are layered and correspond to the network architecture. We shall discuss this later. Suffice it to say now that for the mail service there will be protocols at one layer that are specific to mail which will then use the protocols at a lower layer that are pertinent to managing the traffic through the network. The widely used protocols are the mail-specific **SMTP** (Simple Mail Transport Protocol), and the traffic-specific **TCP/IP** (Transmission Control Protocol/Internet Protocol) (see Tanenbaum, 1996).

TCP/IP facilitates the routing of messages through the network or inter-connected networks and the establishment of a connection for the computer to computer communication. SMTP will use the connection set up by TCP/IP to deliver and receive the mail.

In order to ensure the correct delivery of the mail, each user of the mail system must be given a unique ID and that ID must be used to locate that user. Since mail users would like a global delivery service, it follows that the identification and addressing must be worldwide. This is afforded through the Internet's Domain Name System, **DNS**.

In DNS users exist in regions called domains. User IDs (also called user names) are unique within domains and the user's address is then a domain name. Domain names and the corresponding computer addresses must be registered with DNS. The naming system is hierarchical and implemented as a multilevel set of domains (see Figure 1.4). For example, cs.ucl.ac.uk is a valid domain name in DNS. The highest level domain is on the right. Therefore cs.ucl.ac.uk indicates that the domain cs.ucl.ac.uk is in the domain ucl.ac.uk which is in the domain ac.uk which is in the domain uk. That is, the Computer Science department of University College London which is an Academic Institution in the UK.

Therefore the email system must interact with a naming system in order to associate a user with an address. How is this interaction done? Where is the naming system? How is the register of names and addresses maintained? How does one ensure the integrity of the entries? Are the software modules replicated,

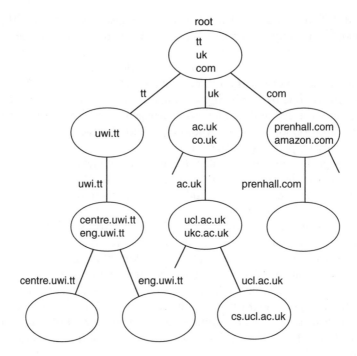

Figure 1.4 An example of a hierarchical domain naming system.

and if so, how are operations coordinated? These are some of the distributed system issues that will be addressed in this text.

1.2.2 News

If there were no news delivery systems, then a scheme that could be employed would be to mount all the news on a massive bulletin board in the centre of town, and around the board would gather all who wanted to read. Having put this basic bulletin board system in place, we can then think of ways in which it can be improved.

We can divide the news into sections (or newsgroups) and allocate a part of the board to a particular section. We can accommodate the expression of opinions on news items by allowing readers to mount their responses on the very bulletin board. Then to deal with the increasing popularity of this system, we can build more bulletin boards and locate them at strategic locations around the country. Since all the users may still like access to all the news, we will then have to devise a way of ensuring that all the boards carry the same (or very close to the same) displays.

This bulletin board description is a fair comment on how an interactive news service is managed over our computer networks. The bulletin board will be maintained at a specified computer to which access will be afforded for mounting news, opinions, responses and of course for passive reading. In order to increase the availability, to reduce flooding of a centralized board and address other performance issues, the bulletin board can be replicated fully or partially across several computers.

The Internet's netnews is used by millions around the world. Replicated bulletin board type systems are maintained and access is facilitated through the use of the news protocol **NNTP** (Network News Transport Protocol). In keeping with the layered structure in the network architecture, NNTP makes use of the TCP/IP protocols for routing and transmission through the networks.

1.2.3 File transfer

The file transfer service allows the copying of a file from one computer on the network to another. **FTP** (File Transfer Protocol) is the widely used file copying protocol which copies files across the Internet. To copy a file one must specify origin and destination parameters. With respect to the origin one must at least identify the file, the directory in which it is stored and the computer at which it is located. For the destination one should also specify a directory and, if desired, a new name for the file.

The FTP service, if available, can be invoked usually by clicking on the *ftp* icon or with a

ftp hostname

command, where hostname is the Internet's DNS known name of the remote computer from which the file is to be transferred. The FTP program will then prompt the user for the details specific to the file(s) to be transferred.

1.2.4 Remote login

The remote login service allows a user to login to a remote computer and execute specified computational tasks. This facility must be restricted to users with valid accounts on the remote machine or access will be allowed only to tasks or files classified as public. **Telnet** is a widely used program for remote login to computers on the Internet.

1.2.5 The World Wide Web

The World Wide Web (WWW or usually just the 'Web') is easily the most dominant information resource and accessing capability on the Internet (Handley and Crowcroft, 1995). With the Web one can visit many sites on the Internet (familiarly referred to as navigating), and select material for quick perusal (usually called browsing). One can then decide whether to download the material or not. It is customary in the Web folklore to refer to navigating and browsing as 'surfing'.

The Web is supported by client–server architecture which is one of the key software design models in distributed systems. The client side of the Web allows users to access the information maintained and supplied by the Web servers. These Web servers are often referred to as Web sites, which provide the information in sets of Web pages.

The data in Web pages is written in a language called **HTML** (HyperText Markup Language). HTML is an adaptation of the ISO SGML (Standard Generalized Markup Language). Hyper indicates that the text possesses additional functionality. A major additional function is the facility to follow links from one hypertext page to another. These links can take you to other Web sites. The page is located by using its **URL** (Uniform Resource Locator) which provides global identification and the address of the page. Some example URLs you might want to try are

```
http://www.yahoo.com
http://www.pearsoned-ema.com
http://www.cs.ucl.ac.uk
http://www.dmcs.uwi.tt
```

HTTP (HyperText Transfer Protocol) is the protocol used for the transfer of the HTML pages. The Web clients send HTTP requests to the Web server which can respond by using MIME to deliver the HTML pages. Dynamic updating of the Web server is also facilitated by HTTP.

One of the latest features of the Web is the facility to download program code from a Web site for execution, at once, on the requesting machine. In so doing, computer resources needed for computation, audio, animation and so on can be obtained at the client machine. This increases the interactive capability of the system, since it is no longer necessary to produce the finished product at the server and then ship it to the clients, but rather the server makes the program available to the clients at which location the products can be finished.

For example, let us assume that Newhomes Company has a number of basic home designs which they want to show to the public. In addition, after selecting a basic model the client is allowed to make slight modifications. The model construction program with interactive capability to accommodate the modifications could be stored at the Web server, from where it can be shipped on demand for execution on requesting client machines.

The Java language and tools designed at Sun Microsystems provide this type of functionality. Java is an object-oriented programming environment. Objects allow the encapsulation of data and behaviour in one entity – the object. Java provides a secure mechanism to transfer these objects across the Web. A Web page can point to a Java object-oriented program (called an applet). This applet can be located and downloaded and then executed at the client computer.

WWW technology is also expected to benefit from a more versatile markup language, **XML** (eXtensible Markup Language). XML is being specified to accommodate new document-type definitions within the document being transmitted. This would constitute an advantage over the fixed format of HTML.

1.2.6 Multimedia transfers

We have touched on aspects of multimedia transmissions before. Here we merely want to highlight some characteristics and system conditions that are peculiar to systems which provide audio and video transfer service.

Audio and video are very time sensitive. Transmitters and receivers have to be coordinated on strict signalling rates. If this is not done the sound will be incomprehensible and the pictures will be of low quality. Furthermore, the coding mechanisms require relatively long bit sequences to be transmitted in very small intervals of time. Therefore, the demands on the communications and computer support systems will be increased significantly over those demands in text-based systems.

Standards addressing these specific audio and video concerns are available. The Motion Picture Experts Group (**MPEG**) standards are used widely. The primary function in these standards is the compression of the video and audio signals so that they can be accommodated by relatively smaller bandwidth channels. If this compression were not done, then for anyone to receive acceptable quality audio and video a channel with hundreds of Mbps (megabits per second) capability would have to be available right up to the host computer.

The distribution of multimedia services over the networks has raised transmission and communication protocol issues which can be addressed in different ways. The Internet approach has been in the establishment of an architecture called **Mbone** (Multicast Backbone). Multicast facilitates the delivery of a single message to many receivers. Mbone affords the worldwide multicast of live audio and video in digital form. MPEG or other multimedia coding and compression schemes can be used with Mbone. Mbone uses Internet addressing and packet delivery protocols to route the multimedia signals to the multiple receivers.

1.2.7 Distributed computation

A computational task can be divided into a number of cooperating sub-tasks which can be executed at separate computers on the network. The geographically dispersed computers may be located close to the data source, or may be ideally suited, by virtue of some hardware or software resource, to perform some aspect of the computation. For example, the point-of-sale terminals distributed over a chain of outlets of a large department store can compute the total purchase for each customer, update the local branch's inventory, and through a communication link to a central computer, provide timely sales information for management planning and control.

Many large-scale scientific and engineering applications, e.g. digital signal and image processing, computer vision, large-scale simulation, knowledge-based systems, etc., contain procedures that can be executed in parallel. In some cases, it is only by exploiting this parallelism that undertaking such projects becomes feasible. The amount of time that would be consumed if these applications were implemented in a serial mode constitutes a serious constraint. Therefore the opportunity to distribute the computing would be welcomed. Where possible this distribution can be on multiprocessor computers. However, in many cases a network of workstations is more readily available.

A notable system for distributed computation within a cluster of networked computers is the **Parallel Virtual Machine (PVM)**. PVM is a software system that allows concurrent use of heterogeneous computers. It transparently handles key features such as message passing and data conversion for the cluster of machines (Geist *et al.*, 1994).

A distributed application implemented with PVM is first expressed as a number of cooperating tasks. Each task is written as a sequential program in C, C++ or Fortran with embedded calls to communication and synchronization routines in the PVM library. These separate tasks can then run concurrently at separate computers in the network. At each of the target computers must be loaded a PVM module which provides a context for the running tasks and interacts with the network (see Figure 1.5).

There are other significant contributors to this specific area of distributed computation; and happily, a standard for developing parallel applications on networks of workstations and massively parallel machines has been developed. This is called the **Message Passing Interface (MPI)**. MPI facilitates the programming of parallel and distributed applications primarily in C and Fortran 77 (see Dongarra *et al.*, 1996).

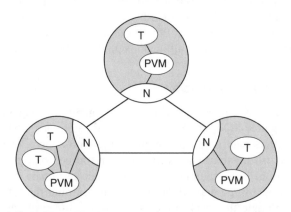

Figure 1.5 Tasks (T) interact with each other in a PVM running context. PVM uses network protocols (N) for communication among the computers.

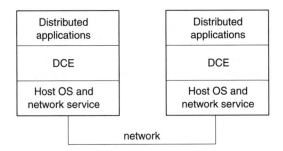

Figure 1.6 Distributed applications use DCE tools to interoperate over
a network of heterogeneous computers.

More comprehensive tools are also becoming available. The **Distributed
Computing Environment** (**DCE**) is a software platform produced by the Open
Software Foundation (now known as the Open Group) upon which distributed
applications can run (Millikin, 1994). Many significant players in industrial
computing have contributed and agreed on DCE, hence DCE tools now enjoy
very wide acceptance.

DCE can run on different operating systems, thus allowing distributed
computation over heterogeneous systems. DCE provides relatively high-level
support for process execution and inter-process communication, and interacts
with lower-level network protocols like TCP/IP to facilitate the computer-to-
computer interactions (see Figure 1.6).

Object-oriented technology is a mechanism for data and procedure abstraction
which facilitates easier reuse of software components in the software development
process. Distributed computation with objects has received tremendous help via a
software architecture that allows the distributed application to use and reuse objects
across the Internet. This architecture is called **CORBA** (Common Object Request
Broker Architecture) and is a product of the **OMG** (Object Management Group).

The OMG is a consortium of computer vendor and end-user companies with
the objective of creating a standard for interoperability across computer
networks. CORBA allows software objects to invoke other objects without
knowing where the objects are located or in what language they are written.

1.2.8 Distributed transaction processing

Distributed transaction processing brings distributed computing into the everyday world of commerce and service-providing agencies. If one needs to pay a
utility bill, withdraw money from the bank, book an airline ticket, make a hotel
reservation or a myriad other such transactions, then distributed transaction
processing can make things easier.

Such systems allow the customer (as in the case of the automatic teller
machines) or a clerk working on behalf of the customer (as at most airline

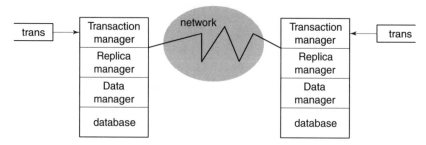

Figure 1.7 Distributed transaction processing systems can handle transactions concurrently at multiple computers linked via a computer network.

reservation offices) to input the transaction on a front-end machine. Transaction management software handles the transaction, ensuring adequate coordination of the other possible concurrent transactions entered at other locations. Data files and databases are usually replicated across multiple computers. This demands careful management of updates in order to preserve data integrity and ensure acceptable levels of mutual consistency (see Figure 1.7).

1.2.9 Electronic payment

Electronic payment is the facility to transfer funds over the telecommunications networks. This facility has been available for some years, but more recently the Internet has provided significant momentum to the development efforts in the field of electronic commerce. The most critical issue is the question of security.

A fundamental model for electronic payment involves a payer, a payee and at least one financial institution (see Figure 1.8). However, the payer or payee may initiate action without the other being involved directly. A digitized payment order is sent to the payee. The payee sends electronic notification to his acquiring financial institution which contacts the issuer institution to effect the money transfer.

Effective electronic authorization and authentication systems must be in place, and there must be quick and efficient accesses to the relevant databases. Data encryption technology must be employed to ensure secure message transfers and to establish the digital signatures for authentication and verification (Asokan et al., 1997).

1.2.10 Distributed real-time processing

Two airplanes are on a collision course and there is a ten-minute interval during which the flight directions can be altered to avoid the tragedy. Assume that there is total reliance on an air traffic controller who, on computing the flight directions, takes just a little more than ten minutes to issue an instruction to

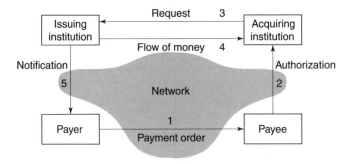

Figure 1.8 Electronic payment allows payment, authorization and notification
to take place securely across communication networks.

change direction. That instruction would be totally useless. This should give one a feel for how critical real-time processing can be.

In real-time processing it is necessary not only to be computationally accurate, but also to meet a strict deadline. Many computerized real-time systems exist in our production and manufacturing plants, in our vehicles, in traffic control, in the military and other walks of life. Indeed, many transaction processing systems possess real-time characteristics. In some systems the penalty for missing a deadline may not be severe. These are usually called soft real-time systems to distinguish them from hard real-time systems where no deadline can be missed without a costly penalty.

It should be clear that there are very high demands on performance and reliability in real-time systems. The basic structure includes some external device being monitored, a sensor for receiving input or signals from the device, a computer for processing, and an actuator to relay responses from the computer back to the device (see Figure 1.9).

Distributed real-time processing arises when there are multiple external devices with dedicated sensors, actuators and computers connected via a high-speed network cooperating in monitoring a single logical domain, such as, for example, a nuclear power plant or fly-by-wire aircraft (see Figure 1.10). Often it is good practice to include a number of redundant units in order to improve fault tolerance.

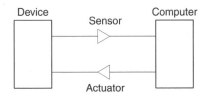

Figure 1.9 A computer is used to monitor a device in real time.

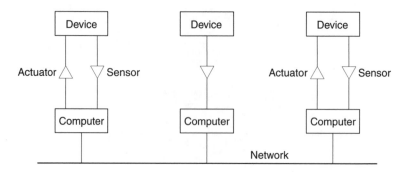

Figure 1.10 A distributed real-time system can monitor many devices via cooperating computers linked by a network.

1.3 Issues

In order to provide these services in an efficient and effective manner, expert attention must be paid to a number of issues. Some of these issues have been hinted at in the preceding discussions and others may have arisen as questions in your mind as you read through the list of services. The following are highlighted.

1.3.1 Naming

The creation and management of names are key issues in the design of distributed systems. Names must be given to the users, to the processes which they generate or invoke on the computers, and to the resources (hardware and software) which they access. The presence of the network increases the volume of the names, and presents a distributed context in which the names can emerge and in which these names must be managed.

A naming scheme must provide the facility to identify entities uniquely across the network. Furthermore, the existence of a name, more often than not, suggests that the location of that named entity is also required. Therefore, the naming scheme should, in some way, be associated with an addressing mechanism.

1.3.2 Sharing

Sharing of resources is one of the main attributes of a distributed system. This is not a new issue. This has been an area of concern since the early days of multiprogramming operating system design. Therefore many techniques exist to address this matter. The concerns include, in the main, authenticating users, providing access rights, scheduling, coordinating and synchronizing access, and resolving conflicts.

1.3.3 Availability and reliability

Availability is a measure of the ability of the system to deliver acceptable service whenever there is the demand. Reliability is a measure of the correctness with which the system delivers. In some cases a system may deliver incorrect output. However, depending on the circumstances the service may still be considered acceptable and therefore available. These standards must be defined for the distributed system and the performance must then not be found wanting. The interconnection of multiple hardware and software resources afforded by distributed systems should be fully exploited in order to ensure acceptable levels of availability and reliability.

1.3.4 Replication

The maintenance of copies of information at separate computers is a useful characteristic of distributed systems. This replication can contribute positively to the availability and reliability of the system. When one copy of information is inaccessible another one might be available. Replication can improve load sharing, reduce communication costs and improve response times. However, these benefits do not come without a cost. One significant cost item is the processing overhead that is required to maintain an acceptable level of mutual consistency among the copies. Replica management has attracted a sizable body of procedures and algorithms, all addressing the integrity, consistency, concurrency and availability concerns.

1.3.5 Privacy and security

Protection against unauthorized access, corruption and loss of material must be assured if distributed systems are to enjoy widespread adoption. The security problems are compounded by the network access. In some sense one might be able to say that networking makes the computer vulnerable to a 'world' of attacks; and based on what has been reported those attacks have been fast and furious.

Many strategies have been implemented in an attempt to provide confidence to the users of computer networks. Some of these (passwords, access control lists, capabilities, memory protection) have been used effectively in stand-alone systems, while others (like firewalls) have arisen within this new networking culture.

1.3.6 Communication

The physical links among the computers provide connectivity. However, effective communication is achieved only if what is relayed is timely and makes sense to the receiver. To achieve this several communication protocols have to be established. We have been introduced to the layered concept in computer network architecture. Most of this architecture is implemented in the software, which means correct algorithm development and coding. The interoperability objective can be achieved only by following accepted standards. It is usually good practice to follow the more widely accepted ones. For example, many distributed systems let their software modules communicate via **Remote Procedure Call**, while many others use a **Message Passing** protocol.

1.3.7 Concurrency and synchronization

Time sharing has always been viewed as a useful feature of computer systems. With single processor systems this means switching the processor among different executing tasks on a continual basis. Multiprocessors afford the parallel execution of these tasks. In distributed systems there are even more opportunities for concurrent processing. Where concurrent processes share resources conflicts can arise. These conflicts can generate corrupted information and inconsistent states. It is therefore sometimes necessary to synchronize these interdependent activities. This often results in the enforcement of mutually exclusive access to resources for certain periods of time.

1.3.8 Time and coordination

The synchronization of interrelated activities may at times have the objective of establishing some order. That is, it is compulsory that certain actions precede others. For example, on an interactive bulletin board it will be unacceptable if some sites see responses to an earlier message before they have seen the original message. Such situations are quite possible due to the vagaries of network communications. The coordination of tasks based on some notion of time is therefore an important concern. Agreeing on what time it is at some instant is an interesting problem in distributed systems.

1.3.9 Fault tolerance and recovery

Distributed systems are not exempted from faults and failures. Integral to the design, then, should be mechanisms to survive most of these. Levels of tolerance must exist which hide many faults from the users, and in response to other faults provide acceptable but reduced service. Strategies that have been employed use a range of techniques including redundant elements, logging schemes, back-ups, time-outs, retransmissions and so on.

1.3.10 Scalability

When designing a distributed system some environment for its installation is usually in view. The environment as currently visualized would dictate certain physical parameters, i.e. size of rooms, geographical expanse, number of users, number of computers, and so on. However, an effective distributed system should not target a static configuration. It should be able to accommodate expansion as well as reduction easily. Furthermore, not only should it be able to cope with planned changes, it should also be able to operate acceptably when components are removed or develop faults without warning. Moreover, with the present technological trends, many distributed systems should be catering for applications with infinite users and resources.

1.4 User–system interface

When we speak of user here we are considering the end-user, the one who consumes the service provided by the system. A distributed system allows this end-user to move from computer to computer and receive the same level of service. Therefore one of the attributes of a distributed system is that it should look and feel the same at all the host computers or front-end machines involved. It will therefore not be necessary for users to familiarize themselves with a different interface as they move from computer to computer. This does not mean that the interfaces are identical in every respect.

Although this similarity is afforded, a user is not prevented from customizing the interface on his computer to satisfy a personal need or fancy. However, if the system is expected to be used by the general public (as with, for example, automatic teller machines), it would be quite foolhardy to present interfaces that are quite different.

The design of the interface will involve the format of the screens (or windows), the use of menus, icons, text-based prompts and commands, and the provision of keyboard, mouse, mouse pads and or other external interface devices that are appropriate. One can try using any of the services outlined above wherever it might be convenient and see how things change or remain the same as one moves from machine to machine.

1.5 Summary

Computer networks allow the sharing of computational resources in real time across physical environments that range from a small room to the entire globe. The difference in area that is covered is captured in the common labels that are used for these networks. These labels are LAN (Local Area Network). MAN (Metropolitan Area Network) and WAN (Wide Area Network).

A distributed system harnesses the computational power of multiple computer systems on a network in order to provide a very useful array of services. The users can access the service concurrently at several different computers on the network. Some of the services provided by distributed systems include email, file transfer, distributed computation, distributed transaction processing and distributed real-time systems.

Many of the services are supported by systems which employ widely used, standardized tools. Some example tools are network protocol suites like TCP/IP, SMTP and Mbone, and software development tools like PVM, MPI, DCE and CORBA. Special attention must be paid to certain technical issues in order to ensure that the distributed system performs well. These issues range from identification and addressing to fault tolerance and recovery.

Therefore we should now have an appreciable understanding of what a distributed system is, what it can do and what the primary concerns are for the designer. We shall move next to look at some major application areas and at the internal structures which give life to these systems.

1.6 Questions

1   What is a distributed system?
2   What is a computer network?
3   What is the World Wide Web?
4   What is object-oriented technology?
5   Name some of the services that a distributed system can provide.
6   Indicate some of the key issues that are to be considered in the design of a distributed system.
7   Computer networks provide opportunities for the exchange of information and the sharing of resources. Suggest some reasons why, in spite of these privileges, there might be some reluctance to linking one's computer to a computer network.
8   Why should the user–system interface with the distributed system remain similar across user computers?
9   Suggest organizations other than the banking industry that you think can benefit from a distributed system.
10 A computerized Student Registration system is to be designed for a large university. What services should this system provide? Should the system be distributed? Why?

CHAPTER 2

Major application areas for distributed systems

In Chapter 1 we discussed a number of services that are supported by distributed systems. From a system design point of view these services can be provided in different ways. For example, a system can be designed to offer a single service, e.g. mail; or one system may offer several services, e.g. mail, file transfer and remote login. Furthermore, systems may be designed to run on top of another system, e.g. the command shell runs on top of the operating system; or systems may interoperate through shared resources.

A common and useful approach to distributed system design is to develop main basic systems which harness the underlying resources, facilitate interoperability among these systems, and provide a wide range of services to the users (see Figure 2.1).

Examples of these major systems are distributed file systems, distributed database systems, distributed real-time systems, distributed multimedia systems and distributed operating systems.

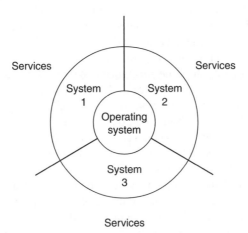

Figure 2.1 Different systems, supported by the operating system, combine to provide a range of services.

- Distributed file systems can support all the file related services like file transfer, news, the Web, etc.
- Distributed database systems can support the Web, transactions, electronic payment, real-time, multimedia, etc.
- Distributed real-time systems can interoperate with the distributed database as well as provide management and control in hard real-time systems.
- Distributed multimedia systems cater for the special needs of audio and video transmissions.
- Distributed operating systems can provide the basic software platform upon which all the other systems can run.

We shall now look at each of these in turn. The matters that will be discussed will have bearing even on other distributed systems to which we will not refer directly. You will see how the issues introduced in Chapter 1 re-emerge within these specific contexts. However, any elaboration on significant, common principles will be done in following chapters.

2.1 Distributed file systems

The need to store and retrieve large volumes of data is widespread. One of the greatest appeals of computerization is the ability to cope with the vast data storage and retrieval needs that exist almost everywhere. Hence techniques to offer such a facility at minimum cost and acceptable speed have to be developed and continually maintained. The distributed file system is one of these techniques. We assume that you have had a previous introduction to file systems. In addition to those usual file management functions performed by filing systems, the distributed file system must cater for the problems introduced by network access. The distributed file system is a distributed system, as defined in Chapter 1, with the specific task of providing network-wide file service (Svobodova, 1984).

A fundamental objective of a distributed file service is to provide secondary storage on large-capacity, high-performance disks for files accessible by the users spread over the network or internetworks. Levels of service which can extend to a full-scale file system can be built upon this basic facility.

The users of a file system should be able to create, read, write and delete files. In addition, they should enjoy some level of privacy and security and the privilege of sharing files with other users. Furthermore, the users will be concerned about aspects of performance such as response times, availability and reliability.

Traditionally, all of these facilities were implemented at a local site and there are still some advantages in this approach. Such an implementation gave more control and hence more physical security and more resilience to failures. However, the user had to be satisfied with what was available locally. The distributed file system has changed this. Now there is the question of how to make the best use of local and remote resources.

2.1.1 Structure

The **client–server** model is usually employed as the software structure for a distributed file system. The modularity inherent in this model affords easy scaling. The server can be viewed as the software module that manages a shareable resource. Often the resource resides at one location in the network and the server is run on the computer at which the resource resides. The server must offer an acceptable level of service to all the users of the network. The mechanics of accessing this server are hidden from the network user by interface software which resides at the separate computers. This interface is usually referred to as the **client** (see Figure 2.2). In the distributed file system the resources to be managed by the server will be the files, directories and other control information, and the storage media.

One way to provide service when all the files are held at a remote location is to allow only file transfer activity. Irrespective of whether the user wishes to use the entire file or merely to read a single data item in that file, the entire file must be **downloaded** to the client machine. All other file activity – read, write, append, etc. – is performed at the local station. The file server behaves like a repository for the storage and retrieval of files.

This approach contains some limitations, chief among them being the restriction of file size by the availability of storage at the client machine. Another setback is that even a small update would necessitate at least two file transfers – remote to local followed by local to remote. However, this type of service can be suitable where the files are programs which can be loaded and run on demand at different stations.

Furthermore, downloading the entire file on the initial access can increase the throughput time on subsequent accesses. It also simplifies the server design since it reduces the level of detail required in order to control the files. Therefore it might be desirable to introduce **caches** at the client machines to temporarily store the opened files.

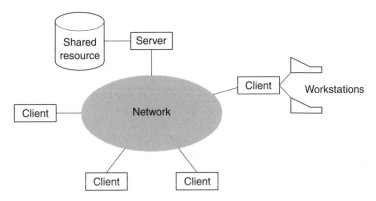

Figure 2.2 Server manages a shareable resource used by a number of clients.

This, however, means that the clients will have more work to do, since (among other things) they must now employ decision-making algorithms to determine when requests should go to the server or stop at the client. There is also the overall cache consistency problem (see Section 4.3) that arises if concurrent access by multiple clients is allowed.

Another approach to client service would be to allow access to files at a page/ block, record or even word/byte level. Access to individual pages or blocks would mean that the client can fetch at one time some number of records determined by the block size. This can be extended to the support of **virtual memory** systems for the client machines.

Access to individual records would require the server to extract the appropriate record from its block before transmission. Word or byte access allows manipulation by the client of the individual fields of a record, which can be used to accommodate a distributed database system. However, it might be more cost-effective to transfer the entire page rather than a record or byte.

A corresponding increase in the size of data areas allocated to address resolution may come with the decrease in size of the unit of access (file, page, byte). However, with concurrent access being supported, the smaller units of access permit wider sharing and so increased availability of the resource which can generate better response times.

If the unit of access is a file then it may be necessary to let only one user access that file at a time unless multiple copies are distributed, in which case there can be simultaneous access but to separate copies. If the unit of access is a part of the file, e.g. a page, then it is possible to allow parallel access to the file where each user has a separate page. Of course, it must not be forgotten that the entire file may be less than a page. However, there will be greater demands on the file server system for adequate concurrency control mechanisms to prevent deadlocks and avoid corruption of file contents.

The use of the client–server structure introduces the notion of division of labour between clients and server. An acceptable organization is that of a number of clients, each with its own file system, superimposed upon the file storage/ retrieval facilities offered by the server (see Figure 2.3). In this organization, the

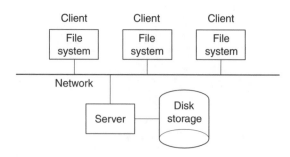

Figure 2.3 Each client of the file server has its own file system.

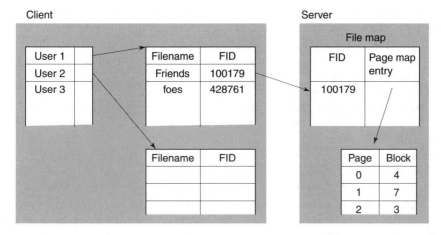

Figure 2.4 Client maintains file system to map local textual names onto global FIDs.

client will have a directory system to allow the correspondence between the users' textual file names and the global unique file ID (FID) (see Figure 2.4). The client will also have some responsibility for the control of access to these files. The file server manages the allocation and deallocation of disk storage, and provides an interface for client–server communication. This interface will include **primitive** commands (e.g. create file) and some communication protocol. Allocation of storage to files is usually dynamic with space allocated as the files grow.

Global file naming is done at the server level. In response to the client's create file request, the file server allocates storage and the unique FID to the file. This FID is given to the client for all future reference to that file. The client must ensure that only authorized users can use this file by controlling access to the FID. If the server allows access to any client in possession of the FID, a client can send the FID of a file to another client, thus permitting access from different machines.

If the file server provides automatic backup and recovery facilities then it may be necessary to categorize files. For example, files can be classified as recoverable, robust or ordinary (Svobodova, 1984). A recoverable file is one for which there always exists an earlier consistent state to which the system can revert when an operation on the file fails. A robust file is guaranteed to survive failures of the storage device and medium. An ordinary file is given no special treatment. Redundancy in the storage of files or parts of a file forms the basis upon which these special files can be supported.

Files are usually stored in non-contiguous fixed-size blocks on the secondary storage medium. The file itself is therefore divided into a number of pages and each page is mapped onto a block. The server maintains a **page map** to point to the blocks in which the pages are stored. There will be an entry in the server's root directory pointing to the page map of each file stored (see Figure 2.4).

In addition to storing the data contents of a file, one must store certain attributes of that file. These attributes – file creation time, file length, time when last modified, etc. – will form the file header which can be stored with the page map. Therefore, access to the header will not necessitate travelling all the way to the actual data blocks.

The unit of access available to the client will determine how much data are stored for mapping the client's logical request onto the physical address. If only file transfer is permitted, then, on the initial request, the server will retrieve the entire file via the page map. If the unit of access is some part of the file, the server must employ some additional procedure to extract the required subrange.

The specification of such a subrange is based upon the client's view of a file at the server level. One approach is to let the client see all files as a fixed-length, contiguous string of bytes or words. The client may then be permitted to access any contiguous substring of words/bytes. The server does the mapping onto the physical storage blocks.

For example, a request to read a sequence of bytes may take the following form:

read-data(FID, no-of-bytes, first-byte-no)

The server must execute some algorithm to find the pages which contain these bytes. As an exercise, you should be able to provide an algorithm to locate the pages and then follow the page map to obtain the appropriate blocks or disk sectors.

The client, on the other hand, may be allowed to divide the file into pages and specify subrange requests within page boundaries. However, different clients may find different page sizes suitable, which presents a problem to the server, and an arbitrary subrange within a file may be preferable. In this case, the paging will be transparent to the client.

The FID can be designed to contain information on the storage address of the file. This means that the **root of the file** (i.e. the location of header and page map) cannot move and therefore must be updated in place. Alternatively, the FID may be completely independent of the location of the file, in which case the additional mapping mechanism is necessary to locate the root when given the FID.

Another form that the relationship between the clients and the server can take is to let the server maintain one global filing system which all the clients must use (see Figure 2.5). In this arrangement, the client does not maintain a local file system. All file commands are channelled to the file server. This approach has been adopted by many small microcomputer LANs.

Moreover, one can have an organization which combines local filing systems at the client machines with a global filing system at the server. In this arrangement the server maintains a hierarchical filing system with root directory, subdirectories and files. The clients can then link their filing systems to the server's filing system. This linking is usually referred to as **mounting**.

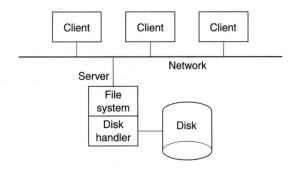

Figure 2.5 All clients use the same file system which is provided by the server.

Mounting allows a client to place a directory obtained from the server at any point in its local hierarchical filing system (see Figure 2.6). It follows, therefore, that clients can have different views of the global filing system. Furthermore, a client can have a filing system which intersects with that of another. Therefore, some mechanism must be employed, either at the clients or at the server, to control access to the shared files.

2.1.2 Issues

We touched on a number of issues pertinent to distributed system design in Chapter 1. These issues are all relevant in distributed file systems. Files must be

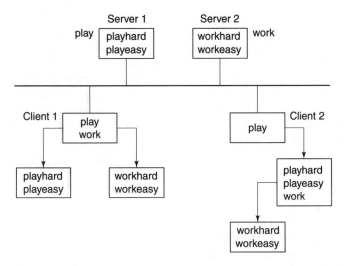

Figure 2.6 Mounting of directories. Server 1 has a directory 'play';
server 2 has a directory 'work'. Client 1 places 'play' and 'work' at the same level;
client 2 places 'work' in a subdirectory of 'play'.

named and addressed in a network-wide context. Files must be shared with local and remote users, and all users should enjoy acceptable levels of availability and reliability.

There is the need for storing replicas of files at different locations. It might even be necessary from a productivity and efficiency point of view to establish multiple cooperating servers. Users must have certain guarantees regarding privacy and security in relation to files stored. Effective protocols must be established for communication between client and server, and where necessary between server and server (Coulouris *et al.*, 1994).

The multiple reads and writes which will occur concurrently demand effective control and synchronization in order to preserve the integrity of the files. There is also the issue of global time and ordering. The effect of failures should always be minimal.

2.2 Distributed database systems

It is clear that an essential ingredient for the successful operation of an organization is accurate and timely information. Furthermore, in many cases there is a global market for certain key elements of information. Computer storage capabilities provide an efficient means for storing the individual data entities from which the information requirements can be met.

In many instances, the volume of data elements may be high, thus placing large demands on computer storage. The same data elements may serve different information applications within an organization. For example, in a manufacturing organization, data on inventory items may be needed for the purchasing, customer-ordering, accounts receivable and accounts payable applications. The earliest computerized business applications usually stored their own copies of the necessary data items, thus generating a great deal of redundancy in data file contents.

Although this practice still exists, an increasingly popular approach is the storage of all the data items pertaining to the whole organization in one central pool called a **database**. This not only serves to remove unnecessary redundancies but also reduces the need for repeated updates to preserve data integrity across the organization (Date, 1995).

Some of the key questions that must be answered when designing an information system are:

(a) Who will be using it?
(b) What data structures will be employed?
(c) How are data items related?
(d) How will the data items be stored?

These factors have all been addressed in database technology and we assume that you have been introduced to the fundamentals of this technology.

Computer networks have created the opportunity to share large databases among many users who may be widely dispersed geographically. A local area network can interconnect the functionally distinct departments of large organizations. Adequate storage capabilities can be allocated to a single site for the purpose of operating a centralized database accessible by all the users of a network.

However, such a centralized arrangement makes the database vulnerable to failures at the site at which it resides. Variable communication delays, biases in the channel allocation method and routing algorithms can render an inequitable service to users of the network. In addition, depending on the demand for service, the centralized resource can suffer periods of saturation which can seriously degrade performance levels.

One solution is the distribution of the database. In this arrangement, the database is divided into a number of cooperating databases, each located at a separate site, and users of the database at any site are allowed to access both locally and remotely stored data. Such a system is called a **distributed database system (DDBS)**.

An organization may contain many branches, as in the banking business. Each branch can store the data elements pertaining to their local customers on site. Therefore, the majority of the transactions should be handled by accessing the local database. However, customers must be allowed the privilege to use the facilities at other branches as well. In such circumstances, it would be useful to permit the remote branch to access a customer's account immediately even though it is stored in an off-site database. Hence, we will have a system where the collection of local branch databases forms a DDBS accessible by all the branches. This is one example of the way in which a database system can be distributed.

A DDBS has a number of advantages over a centralized database system. There is the potential for increased reliability with the spreading of the database over several sites. The database could be partitioned in such a way as to locate sections closer to their areas of highest demand. This can improve transaction processing times. Furthermore, the distributed system can generate distribution of the communication traffic on the network and thus reduce the incidence of saturation at some central site.

Maintenance and upgrading of the database will benefit from the modular implementation of the distributed system. With some degree of replication it is possible to redirect transactions when some site is temporarily off-line. New modules can be added as the need arises.

2.2.1 The distribution problem and pattern

The task of distribution involves deciding where to locate the relations or objects in the database in order to provide the best level of service at minimum cost. In a network environment where transactions at individual sites are functionally distinct (transactions in the personnel department compared with those in the accounts department) or where transactions access mainly local data (local branches in the banking organization), the partitioning of the database may mirror this distinction. However, where the functions are not naturally distinct the partitioning is not as clear cut.

Irrespective of the form chosen for distribution, there has to be some underlying system which supports the storage of these logically related files across the network. In this regard the client–server structure can be employed. It may even be necessary to implement multiple cooperating servers.

There are certain parameters that must be considered when undertaking the distribution of a database. These parameters are:

(a) the volume and activity characteristics of the database,
(b) the number of participating hosts or sites,
(c) the storage facilities at the different sites,
(d) the channel capacity along the communication links, and
(e) the cost factor relating to all aspects of the design.

2.2.2 Volume and activity

Volume pertains to the number of relations or entities, the number of tuples in a relation, and the number of attributes within the tuples. Large numbers of data items will necessitate huge storage capacities.

Activity pertains to the distribution of transactions across the network: what type of transaction occurs where, how frequently it occurs, and the response time constraints on the transactions. The 'type of transactions' depends on the nature of the processing and the database elements needed to complete the transaction.

2.2.3 The number of participating hosts

The number of hosts accessing the distributed database will affect the pattern of distribution. One of the major objectives in the distribution is to provide a high level of availability. Users at a particular site should be unable to perceive delays when processing transactions which require remote access. One solution is to store a copy of the entire database at each site. However, the transaction activity generated by some sites may be so low that this total copying cannot be justified.

2.2.4 Storage facilities

Storing copies of large portions of the database may increase availability. But this incurs a secondary storage cost which the system may not afford. Hence, in order to save on this cost, existing storage facilities may be used which may mean less copying. On the other hand, if replication can be afforded then mutual consistency becomes an issue.

2.2.5 Communication load

In order to minimize the communication load the system should aim to maximize the local processing. This maximization of local processing is subject to the availability, at the local site, of the database fragments that are required.

2.2.6 A pattern

The distribution can assume any of the following forms: *replication, full partitioning, vertical partitioning* and *horizontal partitioning.*

In a **replicated** database each relation or object is stored at more than one location. If each location has a copy of all the relations, the database is *fully replicated.* On the other hand, if each relation is stored at only one location the database is *fully partitioned.*

Vertical partitioning obtains in a relational database where relations are distributed vertically or in columns. In this system, subsets of attributes of a relation are stored at separate hosts. Each host will, therefore, contain some attributes for all the tuples of the relation.

Horizontal partitioning obtains in a relational database where relations are distributed horizontally or in rows. In such a system, subsets of tuples of the relation are stored at separate hosts. Each host will, therefore, contain all the attributes for some of the tuples of a relation.

In the pursuit of greater system efficiency, it may be necessary to subdivide into even smaller fragments of the database.

2.2.7 Queries and updates in a DDBS

Transactions in a distributed environment are of two types: *queries* which involve requests for information, and *updates* which generate changes to data entries in the database. The distribution of the database is aimed at optimizing the transaction processing. The system should provide the best level of service at minimum cost. However, this distribution introduces some complexities in the handling of updates. All copies of segments of the database must reflect the correct state of the database.

2.2.8 Queries

In a distributed environment, either queries can be processed locally or it may be necessary to access remote sites. The need to access remote sites introduces communication costs and can increase response time. Therefore, one of the major concerns in the optimization of query processing is how to generate the least possible traffic on the communication channel. A recommended approach is to divide the query processing into separate phases.

The first phase of query processing can be called the *copy identification phase*. At this phase, the relations or objects involved in the query must be identified. If there is only one copy stored of each entity, one merely has to locate them. If there are multiple copies, it is necessary to make an optimum selection. Although there are multiple copies, they may not all be available. This will condition the selection. So too should the communication distance separating copies of all entities involved in the query. Information on their location could be acquired through some 'dictionary', which may be replicated at some known (possibly all) locations in order to increase reliability and decrease access times.

All the data entries required for processing the query can be transmitted to a single host where all the processing can be done. The large volumes that may be involved in such a transfer make this an unattractive approach. Alternatively, all the processing that can be done at a single host can be done there, and transmission of entries takes place only when a database entry stored elsewhere is needed to complete an operation.

One strategy is to decompose the query into single site subqueries and multi-site subqueries. The single-site subqueries are then distributed to the appropriate sites. Site subresponses to these subqueries have to be coalesced at some predetermined location. Finally, the complete response has to be composed for the destination site. The choice of sites for all these operations may be influenced primarily by the data volumes involved in the transmissions.

As an example, let us refer to the database of relations given in Figure 2.7 and the following query:

Supplier relation

S#	Name	City	
100	JOHN	POS	
200	DOE	NY	

Unit price relation

S#	P#	Price
100	1011	$0.50
100	1300	$1.50
200	1123	$0.60
300	1246	$0.70

Parts relation

P#	Pname	Quant.	
1011	Bolt	400	
1123	Nut	400	
1246	Screw	600	
1300	Nail	500	

Dictionary

Relat.	Locat.	#Tups	T-size
Sup.	Site 1	800	10
Part	Site 2	1500	10
Price	Site 3	10000	3

Figure 2.7 Database of relations.

What are the names of suppliers in New York State (NY) who supply screws at a unit price of less than $1.00?

Assume that the relations supplier, parts and unit price are at the separate sites, site 1, site 2 and site 3 respectively (see Figure 2.8). Assume further that the query originates at site 1. Single relation subqueries can be done at the resident sites, e.g.:

SQ1.   *Find S#, supplier name where supplier city is in 'NY'; at site 1.*

The result of a selection is the relation

   SR1 = (200, DOE, NY, ...)

SQ2.   *Find P# where pname = 'screw'; at site 2.*

The result of a selection is the relation

   SR2 = (1246, SCREW, 600, ...)

SQ3.   *Find S#, P# where price < $1.00; at site 3.*

The result of a selection is the relation

   SR3 = (100, 1011, $0.50)
         (200, 1123, $0.60)
         (300, 1246, $0.70)

That is the easy part. Now on to the two relation subqueries.

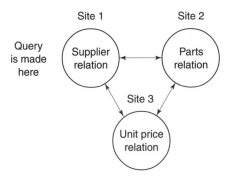

Figure 2.8 Three relations of DDBS at separate sites.

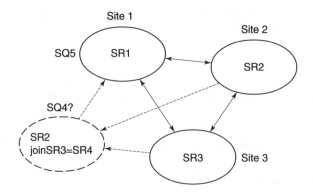

Figure 2.9 The question is where to perform the join operation.

SQ4.   *Find S# for suppliers who supply screws with a price < $1.00.*

Here we need inputs from site 2 (SR2) and site 3 (SR3). There is a choice between doing the join at site 2 or site 3 or even at site 1 (see Figure 2.9). A recommended strategy is to move the smaller relation. The join produces relation

SR4 = (200, 1246, $0.70. SCREW, 600, ...)

SQ5.   *Find supplier name where supplier is in 'NY' and S# equals those obtained from response to subquery SQ4.*

Since the response is needed at site 1, the response from SQ4 could be transferred to site 1 (see Figure 2.9) where the join and projection to determine the supplier name could be performed.

From this example it is obvious that the join operation is the most critical. Techniques must be employed to optimize the critical operations. One approach is to use the *semijoin* operation.

The semijoin from relation R to relation S on the attribute A is equivalent to the join of R and S followed by a projection back onto the attributes of S. In other words, the resulting relation is the same as that obtained after a selection from S of those tuples which have values for attribute A that match values of attribute A in relation R.

Another factor that must be considered is the distribution of processing power over the network. The fact that processing can be done at a local site may reduce the communication load, but at the same time it increases the CPU load at that site. How well can this site deal with an increase in its processing load? Does this operation have high priority or would it have to join a long queue? Since indeterminacy in the response times cannot be accommodated in the DDBS, it may be necessary, at times, to ship the database entries to another site for the processing.

2.2.9 Updates and integrity

Two major conditions in a distributed database system make the processing of updates a difficult task. One is the fact that concurrent transactions are allowed. If two updates are being processed for the same data item fields at the same time, what is the final state of the area updated? The other condition is the possible existence of multiple copies of sections of the database. The contents of the replicated portions must be consistent. These issues are common to other distributed systems where writes are allowed. Therefore we will discuss these matters under Replication in Section 4.4, Concurrency in Section 5.2 and Transactions in Section 6.2.

2.3 Distributed real-time systems

Distributed real-time systems facilitate real-time transaction processing, electronic payment, real-time process control, physical system monitoring and a range of other related services. As was indicated in Chapter 1, some real-time systems carry a very severe penalty when a deadline is missed.

The objective is that these systems provide accurate and timely information at all times. Each component in the system must therefore meet a high standard of availability and reliability. This means that there will be stringent requirements on computer processing power, memory capacities, communication bandwidth and the software modules. The specific service or range of services that will be provided by the system must be used to formulate the particular requirements specifications.

Some of the major parameters that should guide the formulation of the specifications are:

(a)   In what type of environment(s) will the system be located?
(b)   What geographic range will the system cover?
(c)   What is the nature of the communication traffic that will be generated?
(d)   What is the nature of computer processing that will be demanded?
(e)   What communication and other infrastructure are already in place?

2.3.1 Environment

The type of environment determines the type of interfaces and the category of equipment that should be used. Some environments can be considered to be less demanding (or less hostile) than others. A nuclear power plant, a busy factory floor and a geriatric home each provides a different type of challenge.

2.3.2 Geographic range

The extent of the area covered determines the type of network technologies that should be employed. There may be choice between wired as opposed to wireless systems. Small areas can be handled with local area network technology, while metropolitan or wide area network technologies will be required for the larger expanses.

2.3.3 Communication traffic

A good assessment of the expected communication load will allow a good choice of communication bandwidth and signalling techniques. Sometimes it will be necessary to obtain dedicated channel capacity rather than use shared, public facilities. Furthermore, the communication load can be a factor in deciding the level of replication of servers and other resources. Any specifications will take into account the current position regarding infrastructure.

2.3.4 Computer processing

This will relate to the databases and other files that are to be accessed, and the type of computations and/or data manipulations that must be performed. In this regard a number of the issues discussed under distributed databases will be pertinent.

Time is of the essence in these systems. It is even more critical in hard real-time systems. In monitoring a device (see Figure 1.9), the basic concern is to respond to certain state changes in that device, for example an increase in temperature, a change of direction, a drop in height, and so on. It is necessary that the correct response be made within a strict deadline.

In the distributed system where the monitoring is distributed over a network of several computers, the clocks must be synchronized. No one can be allowed to be out of step. The devices can be tested periodically to determine state change. In this arrangement the monitor procedure(s) will be triggered on a specified time interval. The possible behaviour of the system, up to the worst-case situation, could be predetermined within some probability, and the appropriate sequence of operations scheduled for immediate invocation on the observation of a particular change of state.

In such time-triggered systems the choice of the time interval is critical. If it is too short there will be unnecessary testing overhead. If the system is dedicated exclusively to real-time monitoring and control, it might not be immediately obvious why over-testing can be a problem. However, it should be noted that there will be increased traffic on the network (which can mean more bandwidth and/or better communication protocols), and shorter time intervals for handling interrupts and executing other computing processes (which can mean more processing power and/or greater programming skills). If the time interval is too long there can be failure to respond in a timely manner to some event.

The need to build in to the system sufficient redundancy in order to tolerate failure cannot be over-emphasized. Furthermore, maximum affordable delay time on message transmissions and responses must be determined and alternative procedures established to be executed when these latency thresholds have been reached. These parameters and procedures will be largely system specific (Tanenbaum, 1995).

2.4 Distributed multimedia systems

Multimedia transfer systems provide computer storage and retrieval, and network transmission capability for a wide range of information types. However, primary attention is given to the issues associated with audio and video transmissions. The audio and video signals must be encoded in digital form at the source before transmission. Corresponding decode operations must be performed at the receiving sites.

2.4.1 The signals

The audio signals require sampling rates in the range from 8000 times per second (in the telephone system) to 44 100 times per second (as in audio CDs). Whereas the speech signals can be transmitted at 56 or 64 kbps, stereo quality audio CD would require up to 1.411 Mbps.

Video reception is based on the property that a number of discrete images can be displayed within quick succession without the receiver observing the change from one to the other. In human beings this effect can be achieved by flashing images at a rate of 50 or more images per second. The images in video can be represented as a sequence of frames. A frame is a rectangular grid of pixels where each pixel can represent a colour code.

The quality of the representation is affected by the granularity of the grid and the range of colours that can be coded into a pixel, i.e. the number of bits allocated to a pixel. A single-bit pixel can provide only two colours – black and white. Twenty-four bits per pixel with a frame of 1024×768 pixels is illustrative of present high-resolution technology. Transmitting at 25 frames per second would require transmission capacity in excess of 400 Mbps. It should be clear, therefore, that some form of compression is absolutely necessary.

Present coding and data compression techniques provide significant reductions in the storage and transmission requirements. The popular MPEG standards offer multimedia transmissions at bit rates of 64 kbps, 1.2 Mbps, 3 Mbps, 4 Mbps and 6 Mbps, among others, depending on the particular standard and quality of service. This compression is accompanied by correctly synchronized and fast decode functions at the receiver in order to facilitate faithful reproduction of the signals.

2.4.2 Video on demand

Multimedia transmission capabilities support live broadcasts as well as the recording and playback of audio and video material. A hot multimedia application and a good candidate for distributed system technology is **Video on Demand (VOD)**. In a VOD system a VOD server maintains a digital repository of videos which home users, via communication networks, can access and view immediately (see Figure 2.10). The viewers interface with the VOD system through some VOD client whose primary function is the decoding of the signal. The storage requirements at the server will be high. An MPEG-formatted 90-minute movie can occupy about 5 Gbytes of storage, hence the storage for hundreds of movie files will be nothing less than massive.

Concurrent access to the video files must be supported, with a high level of activity being generated on the popular videos. Less popular material would be in less demand (Wang *et al.*, 1997). This suggests that the massive storage must be arranged as a hierarchical structure. A recommended structure includes, from the top level to the bottom, RAM, magnetic disks, optical disks and magnetic tapes (see Figure 2.11).

In order to facilitate the many concurrent accesses, a suitable unit of access (as discussed under file servers) or block size for transmission must be determined. This block is calculated by considering primarily the buffer size requirement at the client that is necessary to drive the decode, display and playback functions. Client accesses are read-only (i.e. no update requests to the server); however, as in the case of the real-time systems discussed above, there are very strict time constraints that must be observed.

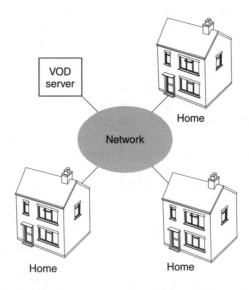

Figure 2.10 Home users can access a VOD server over the network.

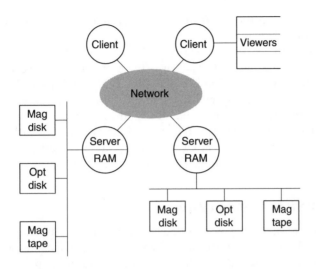

Figure 2.11 Distributed Video on Demand system.

These time-critical concerns must be addressed in the software procedures used for accepting and scheduling requests, and accessing the storage, and by the installation of efficient hardware components. A multiprocessor computer can be employed at the VOD server to handle the incoming traffic, the processing, and output traffic. The accesses to the magnetic disks can be improved by employing Redundant Array of Inexpensive Disk (RAID) technology. With RAID the blocks in a video file can be spread over multiple disks from which these blocks can be retrieved in parallel.

If the VOD server is likely to be saturated with requests then there is the option to replicate the server either fully or partially. The locations of the replicas must be chosen carefully in order to effect a reasonable distribution of processing and communication load. Updates to the replicas would not be a critical issue, since these can be done at set times under management control.

2.5 Distributed operating systems

We assume that you have had an introduction to the fundamentals of operating system design (see Stallings, 1995). Therefore you should be aware that the operating system can be viewed as a resource manager with the objective of providing the best possible service to the users of those resources. The resources usually include processors, primary memory, secondary memory, peripheral devices, programs and data. Many effective strategies have been employed in operating system design for stand-alone computers. Some of these strategies are applicable in the computer network environment. However, the network and the consequent opportunities for distribution, communication and sharing have presented new challenges.

Let us return briefly to the systems outlined above. All of them require the services of the operating system. Hence these systems may be either closely associated with or integrated into the operating system. Distributed real-time and distributed multimedia are specialist systems; therefore it is wise in these cases to use an operating system which is tailored to address their peculiar characteristics. Distributed file systems and distributed database systems are rather general in nature, the former being even more so than the latter. Therefore, more options exist with respect to their relationship with the operating system.

2.5.1 Network operating system

One approach to operating system design for computer networks is to let each host computer have its own operating system managing its local resources, and all interaction with the network will be done through an agent process. Therefore all shared services over the network will be accessible through the agent (see Figure 2.12). This arrangement has often been referred to as a **network operating system**, since it does not possess that quality of transparency that is associated with a distributed system.

It is possible to provide a range of network-wide services through this arrangement. The agent process or module can be configured at one node as a server accepting requests from agent clients at the other nodes. Or an agent can double as both a client and a server at all the nodes. In this way a distributed file service could be provided. The agent server at a node will accommodate file

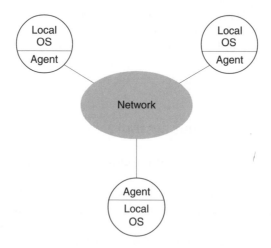

Figure 2.12 Network operating system of agents and
different local operating systems.

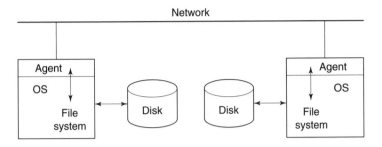

Figure 2.13 Agent as client–server interfacing with local OS file system.

requests from remote clients. Each agent server must be able to interface with the file system of the operating system at its host node (see Figure 2.13).

2.5.2 Distributed operating system

The distributed operating system is a single network-wide operating system. Its implementation involves the replication of the kernel and other modules across all the nodes in the network (see Figure 2.14). Within this structure can be

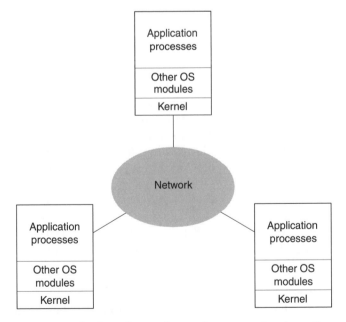

Figure 2.14 In a distributed operating system computers have the same OS kernel and a number of other OS modules from a homogeneous network-wide operating system.

incorporated the general distributed services such as file service. The management of processors, memory, programs, other hardware and software will be done in a uniform manner across the system. The operating system manages data storage and retrieval, data and program migration, load distribution, resource allocation, etc., without the user being aware of all the separate processing sites involved.

2.5.3 Issues

In addition to the fundamental operating system problems of concurrent operation, synchronous and asynchronous processing, there are the particular problems of a network environment. The following points are of major concern:

(a) that the integrity of data transferred and stored should be preserved;
(b) that fail-soft operation in the face of possible crashes at remote sites should be ensured;
(c) that a high level of security against unwanted intrusions is provided;
(d) that an overall level of performance (response times, resource availability, etc.) that is acceptable to the users should be offered; and
(e) that growth or shrinkage should be accommodated easily.

These correspond to the issues that we have highlighted before and with which we shall deal in the following chapters.

2.5.4 Threads

Running processes must be able to communicate in a seamless way with other processes running at the same site as well as with those running at remote sites. The **remote procedure call** and **message passing** primitives are two common approaches that have been used. We shall elaborate on these later. In addition to inter-process communication, concurrent execution *within* a process with intra-process communication and synchronization can be a very useful facility. A program structure that has been developed to support this is the **thread**.

A thread is like a mini-process within a process. It therefore defines a line of execution within the process. A process can contain multiple threads executing concurrently (or in parallel on a multiprocessor) within the same address space. The address space is owned by the process. In this arrangement threads can interact with or pass control to other threads within the process without having to relinquish control to the operating system.

Individual threads execute sequentially and can block themselves and signal other threads to begin execution. This allows use of the blocking procedure call mechanism by one thread, while allowing another thread within the same process to begin execution. Hence, there is the facility to enjoy the benefits both of the relatively simple blocking scheme and of the increased throughput afforded by not blocking the whole process.

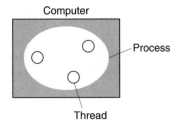

Figure 2.15 Separate threads in a process.

For example, given a server process that must handle requests from multiple clients, the server must continually check its receive buffer to determine whether a request has arrived; if there is a request then some procedure must be started to service the request; if the service requires I/O, e.g. 'read disk', then some disk handling procedure must be invoked.

The checking of the buffer and the servicing of the request can each be allocated to a separate thread (see Figure 2.15). Indeed it is useful to have multiple service threads. When a request is to be serviced, one of the free service threads could be activated. If that thread goes blocked on I/O then another service thread could be activated, provided that there is a request to be serviced.

One may ask the question: could the server process not be designed as multiple cooperating processes and achieve the same result? Yes, but it can be demonstrated that the use of multiple processes would be less efficient. Process-to-process interactions require more operating system overhead than thread-to-thread interactions. Since processes do not share the same address space, they execute in separate environments (or contexts). Whenever one process is stopped (pre-empted) to allow the running of another, the context of the pre-empted process must be saved and the context of the process to be run next must be established.

2.6 Summary

There are several major system areas that are noticeable in the field of distributed systems. Five of these areas are distributed file systems, distributed database systems, distributed real-time systems, distributed multimedia systems and distributed operating systems.

These systems can support all the services that were discussed in Chapter 1. Some services can be provided by these systems directly, or one of the major systems can provide the basic structures upon which other systems can be built. This structural support is true particularly in the case of a distributed operating system.

In discussing these systems it was demonstrated that each possesses some unique characteristics. Distributed file systems address file management issues, while distributed multimedia systems focus primarily on audio and video storage and transmission. However, several key design issues are pertinent all across the board. We met these issues in Chapter 1, we have seen them in this chapter in a general design context, and we shall discuss them in some detail in the following chapters.

2.7 Questions

1   What are the different units of access that file servers have been designed to support?
2   What are the advantages and disadvantages in shipping the entire file to the client on the client's initial request for access to a file?
3   What are the alternatives for file system organization in a distributed file system?
4   What parameters must be considered when distributing a database?
5   What kind of query decomposition can be done when handling queries in a distributed database system?
6   What key parameters should be considered when specifying a distributed real-time system?
7   Why do multimedia transmissions require relatively high communication bandwidth?
8   What is a Video on Demand (VOD) system?
9   Why is a hierarchical storage structure recommended for a VOD system?
10 Indicate the functions of the agent process in a network operating system.
11 What advantages does a thread scheme have over a process implementation without threads?
12 Refer to the Student Registration system in Question 10 of Chapter 1. In which category of major system would this system be placed: distributed file system, distributed database system, distributed real-time system, etc.? What characteristics of these major systems are pertinent to the Student Registration system?

CHAPTER 3

Architecture for distributed systems

In this chapter we shall look at the main architectures that have been adopted in the design of distributed systems. These will include both software and hardware structures. Some of these have been mentioned in the previous chapters within the context of our general overview. It is now necessary to deal with them in some detail.

The overall architecture of the system allows one to form both a physical and a logical view of the system. It provides a background for accurate system specification, which would include the defining of system components and the interrelationships among those components. If there is no clear architecture then understanding the system will be, at best, rather cloudy and its implementation, maintenance and development cannot be well directed.

3.1 Software architecture

The software system lends itself to a global view and to a component-based view. The global view focuses on the overall organization while the component-based view looks at how the parts are structured.

The global structure can take the form of *cooperating processes*. These cooperating processes exchange messages over the network in order to regulate their interrelated tasks. This could be a symmetric arrangement where the processes have equal privileges. This is often classified as a *peer-to-peer* organization. The processes may also operate with a single *master* or *controller* or *coordinator* process which would control the activities of the other processes in a master–slave relationship.

In some distributed applications it is necessary that all the members of the set of cooperating processes be informed about every processing action. This would arise, for example, in the case where the processes are handling the replicas of a database or bulletin board. Message delivery among the members should then always be targeting all the members. Processes forming such a set are classified in distributed terminology as members of a *process group*.

Another form which the global structure can take is the *client–server* organization where there exist dedicated service-provider processes and dedicated service-consumer processes. This has proven to be a very popular architectural model.

The component-based model can be categorized as a *procedure-oriented* model or an *object-oriented* model.

3.1.1 Cooperating processes

Distributed systems facilitate computer-to-computer interaction in the processing and sharing of information. We have highlighted in the previous chapters several examples of these systems. The process is a well-known operating system structure (see Goscinski, 1991). It can be described as an identifiable, logically complete sequence of program code that can be allocated to a processor. Therefore, from this process viewpoint, it is through the execution of processes that users obtain the many services from the computer.

The distribution of computing tasks over the network can be realized by implementing cooperating processes which run at separate computers. These cooperating processes can then be regarded as procedures or tasks in a distributed application. The processes must be identified and registered, and communication among them facilitated and regulated. Programming languages and tools are available for implementing distributed systems as cooperating processes. Some good examples are Ada, CSP and Occam.

Ada

In Ada, parallel strands of activity within a program can each be identified and denoted as a *task*. Tasks can be executed on separate processors or concurrently on a single-processor system (Ben-Ari, 1990).

Tasks are declared within some program unit called its parent. Whenever the parent unit is to be executed, all tasks within it are started and will be executed in parallel unless there are explicit commands to do otherwise.

One task may use services provided by another task within the same parent. Any such service is declared within the server task as an *entry* which can subsequently be called by the other tasks. The server task is delayed until there is a request for service. This delay is implemented through the *accept* statement in the server task. When the server reaches the *accept*, it waits for a request, which is like a procedure call, from the calling task (see Figure 3.1).

This meeting of *call* and *accept* is referred to as a *rendezvous*. The rendezvous action involves execution of the statements indicated by the *accept*. At the end of the rendezvous, the calling task resumes execution and, at the same time, the server task continues execution after the *accept* statement.

The calling task must know the name of the server task and the appropriate entry point, while the server does not have to know who is calling. Therefore, communication is afforded through a known server task which can be viewed as a medium of communication.

Parent

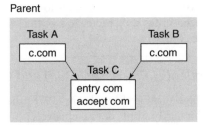

Figure 3.1 Tasks A and B use the services provided by Task C.
Task C waits at 'accept' for entry from calling tasks.

```
task CHARACTERBUFFER is
  entry WRITE (CHAR: in CHARACTER);
  entry READ (CHAR: out CHARACTER);
end CHARACTERBUFFER
task body CHARACTERBUFFER is
  CHARBUFFER: CHARACTER;
begin
  loop
    accept WRITE (CHAR: in CHARACTER) do
      CHARBUFFER := CHAR;
    end WRITE;
    accept READ (CHAR: out CHARACTER) do
      CHAR := CHARBUFFER;
    end READ;
    exit when CHARBUFFER = ASCII.EOF
  end loop
end CHARACTERBUFFER;
task PRODUCER;
task body PRODUCER is
  PROCHAR: CHARACTER:
begin
  loop
    ... produce PROCHAR
    CHARACTERBUFFER.WRITE (PROCHAR);
  end loop;
end PRODUCER;
task CONSUMER;
task body CONSUMER is
  CONCHAR: CHARACTER;
begin
  loop
    CHARACTERBUFFER.READ (CONCHAR);
    ... process CONCHAR
  end loop
end CONSUMER;
```

Figure 3.2 Producer–consumer relationship in Ada.

Figure 3.2 gives a possible Ada implementation of the producer–consumer relationship. The producer writes a character to a buffer, while the consumer reads the character from the buffer.

Communicating Sequential Processes (CSP) and Occam

CSP is a parallel language proposed by Hoare (1978) that permits the specification of programs particularly (but not exclusively) for Multiple Instruction Multiple Data (**MIMD**) machines and computer networks. MIMD systems have many processors each capable of executing its own program on data obtained from a dedicated memory module. Occam is a commercial descendant of CSP. It was designed by INMOS Limited to market the CSP primitives and structures as an effective tool for programming on their transputers. The transputer is a microcomputer fitted with four bidirectional communication links facilitating connection to another transputer or some other device.

In CSP (and Occam), the word 'process' refers to a number of sequential commands which together can be viewed as some subtask or unit of activity. Commands may be simple or structured. Execution of a structured command fails if any one of its constituent commands fails.

A parallel command specifies a number of processes that are to be executed in parallel. All the processes start simultaneously and the parallel command terminates successfully only if and when all the processes have successfully terminated.

Communication between concurrently executing processes in CSP is through *input* and *output* commands. Three conditions must hold before communication can take place between two processes. If process A wants to send output to process B, then:

(a) an *input* command in B must specify that A is the source of the input;
(b) an *output* command in A must specify that B is the destination of the output; and
(c) the target variable specified for the receipt of input must match that specified by the *output* command.

When these conditions are satisfied, the *input* and *output* commands are said to correspond and are executed simultaneously. Hence a process cannot send a message to another unless the destination process is ready to accept it. In this way process activity is synchronized.

For example, let there be two processes, 'receiver' and 'sender', defined as:

```
receiver:: sender ?(x, y)
sender:: receiver !(a+b, c*3)
```

where the process 'receiver' has the *input* command denoted by '?', specifying that a pair of values are to be input from process 'sender' and assigned to

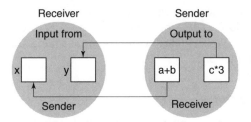

Figure 3.3 Input and output are executed simultaneously
to effect assignment.

variables x and y; and the process 'sender' has the *output* command '!',
specifying that the values a+b, c*3 are to be output to the process 'receiver'
(see Figure 3.3). When process 'receiver' issues its *input* command and process
'sender' its *output* command, they will be executed simultaneously to produce
the effect

```
x  :=  a+b
y  :=  c*3
```

where := is the assignment operator.

Communication in Occam varies slightly from this pattern. Parallel processes
in Occam communicate indirectly through channels. A channel is a one-way link
between two processes. Channels are named and typed, and their names can be
passed as parameters. For example,

```
channel ? variable
```

indicates that a value from the channel is to be input into the variable; and

```
channel ! expression
```

indicates that the value of the expression is to be output on channel. For more
details see Ben-Ari (1990) and Freeman and Phillips (1992).

Tools

Other languages can be used for the construction of cooperating processes
running over a network. To do this some software tool would be required to
facilitate the process interactions. **RPC** (Remote Procedure Call) tools are widely
available. They allow a process to call a procedure in a remotely located process.
The **PVM** (Parallel Virtual Machine) and **MPI** (Message Passing Interface) tools,
introduced in Chapter 1, are available for Fortran, C and C++ programming.
For example, communication primitives like *MPI_Send* and *MPI_Recv* for

sending and receiving messages can be inserted in the MPI-enabled program (see Dongarra *et al.*, 1996). These primitives will be supported by library routines provided by the tool. We shall deal with procedure calling and message passing in some detail in Chapter 5.

3.1.2 Process groups

When the relationship among processes in a distributed system is such that messages must be delivered to all the processes and the activities of the processes must be synchronized in some way, these processes are said to form a group (Birman and Joseph, 1987; Powell, 1996).

In a distributed database system the database might be replicated across a number of sites. In order to preserve database integrity, it would be necessary to maintain a mutually consistent database state at the replicas. This would involve the synchronization of activities at the separate sites and the ensuring of accurate message delivery to all the replicas. These replica managers can then function as a group.

A group of processes is usually formed to improve the availability and reliability characteristics of the distributed service. Processes in the group can be positioned strategically in order to impact positively on the pattern of communication traffic generated by the users of the service and in order to reduce or eliminate the congestion that could arise if a single process were providing the service. Furthermore, the use of multiple processes in a group can facilitate the continued provision of the service in the face of the failure of one or more members of the group.

Group membership

To be in a group a process must be registered as a member of the group. The membership of the group must be known to all the members of the group. A non-member of the group usually has a transparent interface with the group, i.e. the non-member interacts with the group as if it is one process. Sometimes this is facilitated by directing all the traffic to a front-end to the group. At other times different non-members may communicate directly with separate processes (see Figure 3.4). Should this dedicated process go down, another member of the group can be selected to take its place.

A group should be dynamic, i.e. new members may join and current members may leave. Indeed, if a member crashes it cannot send nor receive messages. Therefore, for the duration of the failure, that member should be classified as having left the group, and on recovery it should rejoin the group. Hence, there must be specific protocols for joining and leaving. Since the composition of the group affects message delivery, it is necessary that membership lists be up-to-date and that the membership change be synchronized in some way with message delivery.

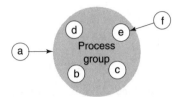

Figure 3.4 Processes **b**, **c**, **d** and **e** are members of a group. Non-member process **a** communicates transparently with the group. Non-member process **f** communicates directly with a member of the group.

Message delivery

In message delivery, a fundamental issue is the network address of the recipients. The membership list of the group and the network name-service facilities would be integral to address determination. If the network provides a physical **broadcast** capability, then group members can listen to the messages in transit and grab those that are directed to the group. In the absence of physical broadcast, the **multicast** of messages to group members would involve multiple point-to-point transmissions. The vagaries of network traffic suggest that no assumptions can be made about correct or ordered delivery of messages. Therefore, the issues pertaining to reliable group communication must be addressed via the adoption of specific group communication protocols.

In group communication it is necessary that a multicast message be delivered to all current members of a group before it is considered a successful delivery. This is facilitated by what are classified as **atomic broadcast** algorithms. Atomic broadcast provides the guarantee that either the message delivery is successful (all live members received it) or message delivery failed (its effects are not seen anywhere).

It may be necessary at times to maintain a total order on all messages, i.e. all messages are received in the same order everywhere. This would require some global numbering system. The use of the physical clock might seem helpful here, but this is not a straightforward option. Sometimes, total ordering is not necessary, since some messages may produce actions that are commutative, i.e. different relative orderings produce the same effect. For example if message A requested that $100 be credited to account X, and message B requested that $200 be credited to account X, then the order in which these are done is immaterial.

Therefore, in the list of messages, there can exist a sequence which may not require a specific ordering, while there might be a sequence in the list which does require ordering. This ordering is usually a causal ordering. For example, examine the following list of messages:

1   Read file *master*
2   Add 100 to *account-X*
3   Read file *account-Z*

4   Create file *account-Y*
5   Add 200 to *account-X*
6   Add 300 to *account-Y*
7   Delete file *account-Y*

If we take these messages at face value it will be quite reasonable to assume that messages 1, 2, 3 and 5 can be done in any order. However, message 4 must be done before message 7. Messages 4 and 7 must be causally ordered to reflect that 4 must happen before 7.

Several protocols and algorithms exist to facilitate ordered message delivery. The ISIS toolkit (Birman and Joseph, 1987) for process group implementation enjoys relatively wide acceptance. We shall look at some ISIS techniques in Section 4.4.

3.1.3 Client–server

The client–server model as a software structure for distributed system design was discussed in Chapter 2 (Section 2.1). In that section it was shown how it can be employed in the design of distributed file systems. Some key issues were highlighted. These included the inherent modularity in the design; the basic roles of server as a producer, and client as a consumer of service; the division of labour between server and client; and the access patterns and other service parameters that can arise given the type of service that is required.

These issues are pertinent to any application that is implemented as a client–server system, and there are, at present, many such applications. Some examples are mail servers, database servers, name servers, print servers, time servers and web servers, just to name a few. Other important issues are how client and server communicate with each other, what guarantees are provided for secure data storage and handling, and how faults and failures should be addressed. Data storage and handling, faults and failures will be discussed in later chapters.

Client–server communication

The process model is often used for client and server implementation. Therefore the communication structures outlined above (e.g. RPC and message passing) often form the software communication subsystem for client–server interaction.

However, the distinctive behaviours of client and server processes demand that a protocol superstructure be built upon the basic communication subsystem.

Two examples of protocol models used are:

(a)   the **three-message protocol** (Mitchell, 1982) in which the client makes a request, the server responds and then the client acknowledges receipt of the response (see Figure 3.5); and

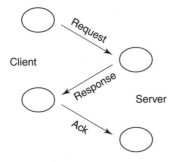

Figure 3.5 The three-message protocol.

(b)   the **single-shot protocol** (Needham and Herbert, 1982) in which only repeatable requests are used (see Figure 3.6).

In the three-message protocol, the client sends the request and sets a time-out interval. If the interval elapses before the response is received, the request is resent. The server also sets a time-out on its response. On time-out expiry, the response is resent. There is a reasonable limit on the number of resends.

The server can throw away the data for a response once it has received the acknowledgement of receipt from the client; and the server can repeat the response if the client duplicates the request. However, the act of repeating the response does not mean that the activity requested has been repeated. In fact, this can corrupt data areas; for example, imagine the result of performing an 'append' more times than the required single operation. Hence the server must be able to detect the duplicate request. A common solution is to number requests sequentially, so that the duplicate will contain the same number as the original.

In the single-shot protocol all requests should generate actions which, when repeated, have the same effect. Such requests are sometimes referred to as **idempotent**. For example, read or write is repeatable, but append is not. It would seem from this that an append can never be allowed. However, this is not the case. Additions can be handled within the context of a set length of the file. The client specifies this set number of bytes before additions are requested. The subsequent 'append' request must not result in this set length being exceeded.

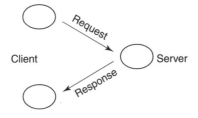

Figure 3.6 The single-shot protocol.

This means that the client interface must be designed so that all requests are repeatable. The server does not save responses for resends. The simple timer expiry can control the request/response activity. The timer starts when the request is sent. If the timer expires before the response is received, the request is repeated.

3.1.4 Component models

At the component level are the programming language structures which underpin the global architectures discussed above. The dominant models here are the *procedure-oriented* and *object-oriented* techniques.

Procedures

The procedure-oriented approach views the computing task or application primarily as a number of steps to be executed. These steps can be grouped logically and then prescribed as procedures which the computer interprets and executes. There are many procedure-oriented languages, but one that has found much favour among distributed system programmers is the C programming language.

The C programming language was designed and developed by Dennis Ritchie at Bell Laboratories (Kernighan and Ritchie, 1978) as a systems programming language for the UNIX operating system. It has been acclaimed for its facilities for controlling the hardware at a low level and for building high level data and control structures. Among its key features are its pointer facility and bit-level manipulation (Deitel and Deitel, 1994; Kalicharan, 1994).

Objects and object-oriented programming

In the object-oriented approach the computer application or system is viewed primarily as an interrelationship among entities. The object is the programming abstraction for the entities in the system. These entities may be hardware resources or software structures. The object comprises not only the data attributes or data fields, but also the set of permissible operations that can be performed on the object. Therefore an object can be specified as a string which includes ID for uniqueness, state determined by its data values, and behaviour determined by the operations. For example:

```
(ID; state: NAME, CITY; behaviour: print[])
```

specifies an object that has name and city values, any of which fields can be printed.

Objects can be categorized by type or class. All objects within the same class possess similar state and behaviour characteristics. For example:

```
class:
supplier = (ID; state: NAME, CITY; behaviour: print[])
```

allows a number of objects of supplier type to exist. The use of the class specifier allows the implementation of **abstract data types (ADT)**. An ADT hides the implementation details of the structure from the users.

The object-oriented model facilitates the building of hierarchical structures through the **inheritance** feature. In particular, inheritance allows the definition of a class based on the definition of an existing class. For example:

```
class:
    part = (supplier; part#; state: PNAME, QUANTITY; behaviour:
    add-to-quantity, subtract-from-quantity).
```

The C++ and Java programming languages are used widely in object-oriented programming.

C++

C++ was designed by Bjarne Stroustrup at AT&T Bell Laboratories in the early 1980s (Stroustrup, 1991). C++ is an extension to C providing object-oriented facilities. It therefore provides a straightforward evolution from C-based applications to object-oriented implementations.

The *class* construct in C++ is used to define new data types, which can then operate as if they were directly supported in the language. Objects can be defined via this *class* construct.

The supplier object indicated above can be defined in C++ as follows:

```
class supplier {
   char id [10];
   char name[30];
   char city[30];
public
   void print(supplier obj);
   };
```

Of significance here is the inclusion of the function 'print' as a member of the object. In C the supplier would have to be declared as a struct data type, e.g.

```
struct supplier {
   char id[10];
   char name[30];
   char city[30];
   };
```

excluding the function 'print'.

The class specification allows the distinction between private and public identifiers. The presence of the keyword `public` in the 'supplier' class indicates that all the identifiers declared before the word `public` are considered private. Private identifiers can only be accessed by functions that are members of the class. In this example only the function 'print' can access the variables in the object. The function 'print' is declared as public, therefore it can be used by any other function in the program.

The inheritance example given above can be expressed in C++ as follows:

```
class part : supplier {
  char part#[10];
  char pname[30];
  int quantity;
public
  void add-to-quantity(int q);
  void sub-from-quantity(int q);
  };
```

Constructors are functions which allow the initialization of an object. A *destructor* is a function that facilitates cleanup when an object is deleted. However, objects can also be implicitly initialized and deleted. Objects local to a block are implicitly instantiated/deleted when a program enters/leaves that block.

Java

The Java programming language was developed by James Gosling and his team at Sun Microsystems (see Arnold and Gosling, 1996; Deitel and Deitel, 1997). While the object-oriented methodology is a principal feature of the language, its use as a tool in Internet Web-page development is one of its strongest selling points. Java programs/applications, called applets, can be programmed into a Web page from where they can be downloaded and run in a secure manner at user machines.

The user machine must have a Java interpreter, which is known as the Java Virtual Machine or JVM (see Figure 3.7). The JVM is the key to Java's portability. The Java compiler translates the Java program into Java bytecodes which form the input to the JVM. This compiled Java program (applet) can be loaded from the local disk or from a remote computer via a Web browser. When the applet is input to the target JVM, the bytecodes are checked to ensure that

Figure 3.7 Java applets can run wherever there is a Java Virtual Machine.

there are no security violations, a running context (runtime) is created and the bytecodes are interpreted for execution by the host computer.

Java was designed around the C and C++ languages. As in C++ the *class* specification is used for creating objects. The state information in the class is defined through *fields*, while *methods* define the behaviour or procedures. The 'supplier' class, defined as a C++ class above, has the same form as a class in Java, with fields *id*, *name*, *city* and a method *print*.

The inheritance feature discussed above is also facilitated. The 'extends' keyword is used in Java to effect class inheritance. For example, the fields and method of 'supplier' can be inherited by 'part' (as above) by prefacing the 'part' definition with

```
class part extends supplier {
```

Java provides a number of other useful features for effective program development. Many of the objects (including strings and graphics) commonly used in applications are already defined in Java class libraries for importation into user programs. Java provides exception handling for catching program errors, garbage collection for better memory utilization, and multi-threading for concurrent execution within a program.

The set of classes available in Java is very rich and is growing at a brisk pace. These classes are divided logically into packages which form the Java API (Application Programming Interface). A hierarchical naming scheme is used to access classes in a package, e.g. `java.awt.Graphics` refers to the `Graphics` class in the `awt` package. The `awt` package (Java Abstract Windowing Toolkit Package) contains classes required to create and handle graphical user interfaces.

Some other examples of Java packages are as follows:

`java.applet`	The Java applet package, which contains the `Applet` class and several interfaces for the creation of applets, and the interaction of applets with the WWW browser.
`java.io`	The Java input/output package, which contains classes that enable input and output of data.
`java.net`	The Java networking package, which facilitates network communication.
`java.rmi`	The Java Remote Method Invocation package, which provides capabilities similar to remote procedure call.

A class can be imported into your Java program via the `import` statement, e.g.

```
import java.applet.Applet
```

imports the `Applet` class from the `applet` package.

A web site's URL can be used as an argument in a method in the Java class `Applet` to access WWW resources, and via Java RMI (Remote Method Invocation) one Java application can invoke methods in another Java application running at a remote computer.

CORBA

CORBA (Common Object Request Broker Architecture) is a product of the OMG (Object Management Group), a consortium of computer vendor and end-user companies working towards interoperability among object-oriented systems. CORBA allows objects to invoke other objects without knowing where the objects are located or in what language they are written.

CORBA supports a client–server form of interaction. Servers possess objects which can be invoked by clients. The interactions between clients and server (see Figure 3.8) are managed and facilitated by the ORB (Object Request Broker). These interactions have properties similar to RPC, which we shall discuss in some detail in Chapter 5.

There can be no meaningful communication between client and server unless they understand each other. The server needs to present its services in a specific way and the client needs to specify its wishes in a compatible manner. This exchange is facilitated through the **Interface Definition Language (IDL)**.

For example, if a server maintains a `Transaction` object and a `TransQueue` object of Transactions (Crichlow *et al.*, 1997), these can be specified for client use in the following IDL statements:

```
interface Transaction {
  attribute string id;
  attribute string type;
  attribute string data;
};

interface TransQueue {
  readonly attribute string name;
  boolean IsEmpty();
  void Append(in Transaction t);
  Transaction Remove();
  Transaction FirstTrans();
  Transaction NextTrans(in Transaction t);
};
```

The `TransQueue` object supports the operations/methods `IsEmpty`, `Append`, `Remove`, `FirstTrans` and `NextTrans`.

On implementation these objects, coded in some object-oriented language (possibly Java or C++), will be managed by a registered server at a

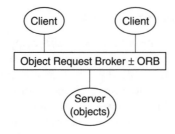

Figure 3.8 The basic CORBA model.

specific host computer. The IDL interface will be mapped onto the target language.

Clients can access the operations in these objects via the interface by first uniquely identifying (or first binding to) the object, and then specifying the target operation. A `bind` statement is provided to establish the bond with the object. For example:

```
Qref = TransQueue._bind(object name: server name, host)
```

allows the object `Qref` at the client to access the operations of `TransQueue` at the specified server. If the binding is successful then the reference `Qref`. `FirstTrans()` is a valid invocation of the `FirstTrans` operation on the remote `TransQueue`.

The ORB provides the transparent interactions between the client and the server. It handles all the intricacies of network communications and the local and remote OS requirements. The openness of a CORBA implementation can be enhanced if its ORB can communicate with the ORB in another implementation. This is possible if the ORBs support the **Internet Inter-ORB Protocol (IIOP)**. IIOP uses TCP/IP connections to facilitate interoperability (see Figure 3.9 and Section 3.2.8).

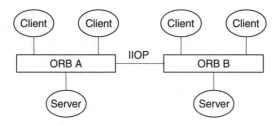

Figure 3.9 ORB A can interact seamlessly with ORB B through IIOP.

3.1.5 Components and frameworks

We have been looking at the structure of the components (individual parts) that make up the global structure of a distributed system. It has been indicated that a distributed system is essentially a mix of procedural and object-oriented techniques. We have also seen how we can import objects from class libraries and, through an IDL, invoke objects owned by a remote site.

It follows therefore that, if we view a component as one or more reusable procedures and/or objects, then, guided by our global structure, a distributed system can be implemented by combining suitable components. This is the type of capability that CORBA and similar technology (Microsoft DCOM, JavaBeans, etc.) are providing.

This has led to the development of (a) component standards which facilitate the integration of the multiple components into the distributed system, and (b) run-time environments which support distributed processing that uses distributed component architecture (see Orfali and Harkey, 1998).

Basic to this architecture is an IDL (Interface Definition Language) as discussed under CORBA. A component must declare itself to the outside world before it can be used. The object model is the favoured architecture. In this approach a component can be viewed, as above, as having state and behaviour. In component terminology state is referred to as 'attribute' or 'property' and behaviour is 'method'. Properties and methods are declared in the interface to facilitate interactions.

Component A can interact with component B by calling one of B's published methods. However, this arrangement produces a rather tight coupling of components. For example, if B maintained a transaction queue, and A wanted to know when the queue was non-empty, then either A would invoke a method in B to determine whether the queue is non-empty, or B would invoke a method in A to indicate that the queue is non-empty.

On the one hand, if A is invoking B, then this can generate repeated attempts, since there is no way in which A can determine whether the queue is non-empty unless it checks. On the other hand, if B does the calling and several components are interested in the non-empty queue, this will generate multiple calls from B to indicate that the queue is non-empty. This has led to the inclusion of another item in a component's interface, i.e. the 'event'.

Events in a component's interface are associated with activities within a component that might be of interest to the outside world. If an application or another component is interested in that event then it must subscribe to it. That is, the interest in the event is registered and whenever the event fires (occurs) all interested are dynamically notified.

'Frameworks' take distributed system design a little further. Rather than making only the components available, one can use the condition that the same (or a similar) application is needed in many different places, and hence build a framework, i.e. a reusable 'semi-complete' application that can be tailored to produce custom applications for the given target environments (Fayad and Schmidt, 1997; Johnson, 1997).

3.2 Network architecture

Distributed systems operate over computer networks. In this section we shall examine this network platform, identifying the key architectural principles which support the present ubiquitous computer-to-computer interactions.

In order to facilitate the design, construction and maintenance of these networks, a layered architecture has been used in network design. For each layer there are the protocols which constitute a framework for the communication at that layer (see Chapter 1). The **International Standards Organization (ISO)** has proposed a standard architecture in order to facilitate the interconnection of different networks. It is a seven-layer model called the reference model of **Open Systems Interconnection (OSI)** (see Figure 3.10).

These seven layers range from the hardware-dependent layer at the bottom of the hierarchy to the user applications environment at the top. They include, beginning at the lowest layer:

(a) the *physical layer* which is responsible for the transmission of the raw bits over the communication channel;
(b) the *data link layer* which transforms the raw bit stream into a string of bits which is free of transmission errors;
(c) the *network layer* which handles the routing within the subnet and determines the interface between the host and IMP;

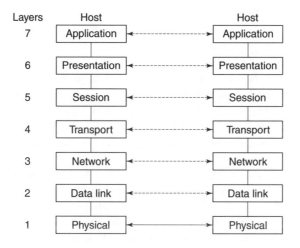

Figure 3.10 The seven-layer ISO–OSI reference model.

(d) the *transport layer* which is responsible for the safe transfer of messages from one application process at a host to another;

(e) the *session layer* which is the layer in which connection is initiated for a communication exercise;

(f) the *presentation layer* which resolves differences in formats among the various hosts; and

(g) the *application layer* where the functions or applications that the user can run are created.

While ISO/OSI embodies the key concerns in network achitecture, its specifications were being formulated at the same time as ARPANET and its successor the Internet were successfully shaping the world of network architecture. Hence the Internet's **TCP/IP (Transmission Control Protocol/Internet Protocol)**, which in many ways is faithful to the principles of ISO/OSI, now dominates. The ISO/OSI protocol reference model still holds its own as a useful vehicle for discussing network architecture, and its specifications continue to enjoy adoption in some mission-critical networks. We shall present briefly this seven-layer model and then show how TCP/IP fits in.

3.2.1 The physical layer

This is concerned with the transmission of strings of bits from one host to the other. It is, therefore, necessary to choose a suitable signalling technique, transmission medium and related equipment to provide an acceptable communication channel. Other concerns would be whether or not to include multiplexing to provide better utilization of the available bandwidth, making the choice between circuit switching and packet switching techniques, and the management of errors.

Digital-to-analog conversion

A wide telephone network is available for speech communications. These speech signals are analog and the telephone network was designed to handle these waves with a frequency range of 300 Hz to 3300 Hz, which is adequate for the human voice. Installing a new network to transmit digital signals over long distances is prohibitively expensive, therefore in many instances the existing telephone lines are used.

Modulation techniques are employed to allow the digital signal to be carried on the analog channel. A device is needed to convert the signal from digital to analog at the sending end and from analog to digital at the receiving end. This device is called a **modem (modulator/demodulator)**. Three common modulation techniques used are **frequency shift keying**, **phase modulation** and **amplitude modulation**.

Frequency shift keying (FSK)

In FSK, the digital signal is coded in frequencies. Each discrete signal value or voltage is converted to a different frequency. Demodulation involves the opposite operation. For the binary signal only two frequency values are needed (see Figure 3.11). One constraint is that, in order to detect the frequency, at least half a cycle must be transmitted. Therefore the time interval, I seconds, between the changes in the value of the signal must be greater than or equal to the time to complete half of the cycle, i.e. half the period, T, of the wave.

Since the lowest frequency used has the longest period, then

$$I \geqslant \tfrac{1}{2}T$$

where T is the period of the lowest frequency, f, that is output by the modulator. This I will be large enough to accommodate the shorter cycles of the higher frequencies. Since the number of signal changes per second gives the baud rate, b, then

$$b = 1/I$$

i.e. $1/b \geqslant \tfrac{1}{2}(1/f)$, therefore:

$$f \geqslant \tfrac{1}{2}b$$

Hence the lowest frequency used must be greater than or equal to half of the baud rate of the data signal.

Phase modulation (PM)

In PM, the signal is coded in **phase changes**. In a phase change the wave retains its shape but there is a shift in its position. Therefore the same frequency is used, but, by dedicating distinct phase changes to particular digital values, the signal can be transmitted.

Large phase changes are used to facilitate detection. At the start of the signalling interval there is a test to determine the extent of change relative to the state in the previous interval. *Differential phase modulation* allows four

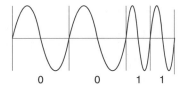

Figure 3.11 Frequency modulation.

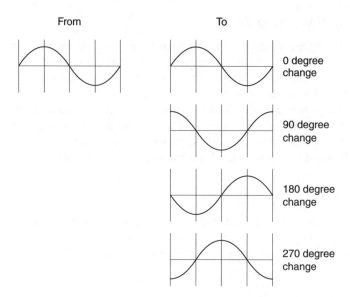

Figure 3.12 Differential phase modulation.

possible phase changes: 0, 90, 180 and 270 degrees (see Figure 3.12). With four such changes, four distinct values can be coded. Therefore two bits of information (00, 01, 10 or 11) are transmitted in each phase change.

Amplitude modulation (AM)

In AM the digital values are coded as specific changes in amplitude (see Figure 3.13). The same frequency is used, but by altering the amplitude, distinct signals can be conveyed. This technique is usually combined with PM to increase the number of combinations that could be represented by the signal change. For example, if each sampling interval can have any one of four phase changes plus any one of two amplitude changes, then eight different digits or three bits of information can be transmitted per interval, i.e. each signal change represents an octal digit.

Since the octal digit is represented by three bits, the bit rate of the modem will be three times the frequency or baud rate of the channel, e.g. a 3.2 kHz

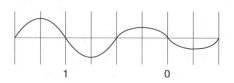

Figure 3.13 Amplitude modulation.

voice-grade channel can be used to transmit at 9.6 kbps. It follows therefore that by employing different combinations of FSK, PM and AM relatively fast modem speeds can be obtained over the available analog channels. Many installations use 28.8 kbps, 33.6 kbps and even 56 kbps modems.

Modulation over non-voice-grade channels

If the analog waves moved at much higher frequencies then the modem speeds could be increased significantly. There are at present two dominant areas where higher frequency analog transmissions are being used to provide faster modems. These areas are **Digital Subscriber Line (DSL)** and **cable modems**. DSL uses the higher frequency bands allowable on the copper phone lines to obtain modem speeds ranging from 144 kbps to 1.5 Mbps. Cable modems, ranging from 500 kbps to 10 Mbps, modulate the digital signal onto the cable TV broadband cable. Transmission media are discussed below.

Advantages in digital transmission

There are many advantages in using a network that can transmit the digital signals. Errors can be monitored more easily, digital processors can be used for aspects of circuit management, and multiplexing techniques are available to permit more efficient use of the network. Therefore, in spite of the great cost, many telephone authorities are changing from the analog system to digital. The analog speech signals can be converted to digital, thus opening up vast opportunities for both voice and computer communications.

Analog-to-digital conversion

With the availability of digital transmission capability and the advantages it offers as a medium for voice communication comes the need to convert the analog signals to digital form. This conversion is done by a device called a **codec** (coder–decoder). The coding technique is called **pulse code modulation**.

Pulse code modulation (PCM)

In PCM the speech signal is sampled 8000 times per second. This sampling frequency, according to the Nyquist theorem, is adequate to capture all the information from the approximately 4 kHz band-limited voice-grade analog signal. Eight bits are used to code each sample, thus producing a 64 kbps of coded voice which can be carried on the digital channel.

The inherent bursty nature of speech and the fact that the analog speech signal changes relatively slowly allow the employment of coding techniques which do not require an eight-bit sampling code. *Differential pulse code modulation* outputs the difference between the amplitude value of the current sample and the previous one. For this scheme a five-bit code is used. Another technique, *delta modulation*, employs a single bit which indicates whether the new sample is above or below the previous one.

Transmission media

Some of the media used in communications are twisted pair, coaxial cable, optical fibers, radio frequencies and communications satellites. A brief intro-duction to these media follows.

Twisted pair

A pair of copper wires is twisted in the form of a helix and one or more of these pairs will be enclosed in a single outer sheath. Twisted pair is generally used for analog transmissions, but has found increased use in digital signalling. It is often the cheapest form of communications media available.

It is still used in many telephone systems where, although a much higher bandwidth can be afforded, it is installed primarily to accommodate the 4 kHz voice-grade signals. Digital subscriber line technology is now being supported on the higher bandwidth by some carriers (see above). Twisted pair is susceptible to a great deal of electrical interference which results in high error rates (about 1 in every 10 000 bits). Furthermore, due to relatively high emissions, it can be easily tapped, which reduces its suitability in areas where security is of major concern.

Coaxial cable

Instead of a pair of wires to conduct the electrical signals, coaxial cable has a solid central copper conductor surrounded by insulating material over which is a conducting tube with an outer insulating layer. Coaxial cable has a lower degree of attenuation at high frequencies than twisted pair cable. A 1 km length of coaxial cable can provide a 10 Mbps data rate when used for digital trans-missions. Higher rates are possible on shorter cable, whilst increasing the length of cable reduces the feasible data rate.

When used for analog transmissions the coaxial cable can accommodate frequencies exceeding 300 MHz. This frequency range makes coaxial cable very suitable for carrying many lower frequency subchannels. Hence its popularity among cable television enterprises which offer tens of TV channels at the same time. Colour TV requires large bandwidth, e.g. 6 MHz, and therefore up to 50 such channels can be easily accommodated on the coaxial cable. Some of the bandwidth on the coaxial cable is now being used to support cable modems (see above).

The coaxial cable's relatively low error rate (1 in every million bits), large capacity and the flexibility it allows in implementation have made it a popular choice for LANs.

Optical fibers

These transmit light rather than electrical signals, which means that this medium is unaffected by electrical interference. There is a central filament (of glass or fused silica) surrounded by a layer of material which prevents the rays of light from reflecting outwards, thus increasing the transmission capability along the length of the filament. It is necessary to convert the electrical signals to light pulses before transmission and to perform the opposite operation at the destination point.

A *Light Emitting Diode* (*LED*) or a *laser diode* is used as the transmitter. Each of these devices emits light pulses when electrical current is applied. A *photodiode* is used for the conversion at the receiving end. The photodiode generates an electrical pulse when light falls on it. The conversions which are necessary at the connection points introduce additional cost and complexity in design. However, the high quality and rates (over 1 GHz or 1 billion Hz) that can be achieved, even in areas of disturbing levels of electrical interference, make optical fibers an attractive option. Error rates for optical fibers have been quoted as low as one bit in a billion.

Radio frequencies and satellite

Messages are broadcast using dedicated channels from the radio frequency band. In using ground-based radio transmission, a few hundred kilometres can be covered. Communication satellites can be used for computer communications over long distances. These satellites can be viewed as large repeating stations which receive the upwardly directed signal and rebroadcast the amplified signal to locations on the earth. These locations may occupy an area ranging from a few hundred kilometres to a major portion of the earth's surface.

Multiplexing

Rather than installing several narrow bandwidth physical channels, one wide bandwidth channel is usually multiplexed, i.e. shared among many users. In order to avoid collisions of messages from separate sources, efficient sharing techniques must be employed. Multiplexing techniques can be categorized as either **frequency division multiplexing (FDM)** or **time division multiplexing (TDM)**.

Frequency division multiplexing (FDM)

In FDM, the frequency range of a wide bandwidth physical link is divided up into several narrower channels. These narrower bandwidth channels will be adequate to meet the transmission requirements of the users to which they are exclusively allocated. Between each of these usable frequency bands there is an unused band which serves to reduce interference across the boundaries of the channels. Since these narrower channels are for the exclusive use of those to whom they are allocated, it follows that these frequencies will be wasted whenever the users have nothing to transmit.

Time division multiplexing (TDM)

In TDM, each user is allocated a time slot during which that user has exclusive use of the entire bandwidth. In its pure round-robin form, it could result in inefficient use of the physical channel. The user can transmit only when his turn comes around and all users get a turn even if they have nothing to send. Therefore, while some users will be allocated time when they have nothing to transmit, other users with heavy transmission loads will have to be satisfied with short transmission bursts and unnecessary waits.

However, some amount of intelligence could be built into the system in order to allocate time slots according to user demand. This would generate a more efficient distribution of time slots. This attempt to allocate time slots on demand is called **statistical time division multiplexing (STDM)**.

Circuit switching and packet switching

The existence of the physical communication link is necessary for the transmission of information whether it is via analog or digital signals. We have seen how the transmission capacity can be shared to permit multiple inputs onto one physical channel. However, there is another dimension to the use of these communication media which we will look at now.

In telephone conversation, there is usually a continuous interchange of information between the speakers, even if at times the responses may merely be grunts or chuckles. In order to accommodate this pattern, the convention is to give the caller and called a complete end-to-end path for their exclusive use throughout the duration of the conversation. This technique is called **circuit switching**. The telephone system uses its switching equipment to establish this dedicated circuit.

Computer communications are essentially 'bursty' (varying amounts at irregular intervals), and sometimes there is no need for an immediate response. A dedicated circuit in a wide area computer network for long periods will therefore mean poor use of the communication resources.

Another approach is possible. When a user at a host has information to send, there is no attempt to dedicate an entire path before the transmission begins. Instead, the message is transferred to the first PSN where it is stored to be forwarded later, on an available link, to the next PSN. This hop-by-hop **store-and-forward** process takes place until the message reaches the destination host. This technique is referred to as **message switching**, where there is no limit on the length of the message *block*, which is determined by the amount of data the user has to transmit.

However, there are obvious difficulties in handling these variably sized blocks. Enough memory must be available at the intermediary PSNs, and short, important messages may have to wait behind long, unimportant ones. It is better to impose a fixed length on the block size. These fixed-length blocks are called **packets**, hence the name **packet switching**. A message is divided into a number of packets and each packet is handled independently of the others.

The division of the message into packets for independent transmission allows more messages to share the network at the same time. This can provide interactive information exchange, a benefit not easily available in the message switching scheme. There must be controls introduced to ensure accurate receipt of the message at the destination host.

Errors

One of the unpleasant facts of life in communications is that errors will occur, corrupting the data transmitted. These errors occur for a number of reasons, including fluctuations in the background noise level of the channel and electromagnetic interference from neighbouring electrical devices.

Methods must be employed to cope with these errors. Techniques used are based on the principle of adding extra bits to the data stream in order to form a code. This code is used by the receiver to determine the accuracy of the message block. There are two major categories into which these codes can be divided: **error correcting** and **error detecting**.

In error-correcting codes there must be enough redundant information so that the receiver can determine both that an error has occurred and what the correct value is. In error-detecting codes, the receiver merely detects that an error has occurred. The correct value cannot be reconstructed. The devices connected to the network should use the same procedure. The code most often used is the **polynomial code** or **cyclic redundancy code** (**CRC**) for which there are international standards (see Section 3.2.2).

3.2.2 The data link layer

Link protocols are concerned with efficient and reliable transmission of information from one **node** (host or PSN) in the network to a neighbouring node. In order for a host to communicate with another, the message will have to pass through the subnet, stopping at several PSNs along the way. Therefore it is essential that each node shoulders the responsibility of error-free transmission to neighbouring nodes. This layer addresses this link-level responsibility which involves the PSN-to-PSN link as well as the host-to-PSN link.

For the purposes of this discussion, it can be assumed that host A has a message to send to host B. Host A is linked directly to PSN A, and host B is linked directly to PSN B. It is sufficient at this layer to imagine the existence of only one link in the subnet, i.e. PSN A to PSN B (see Figure 3.14). The data link

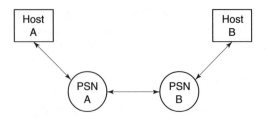

Figure 3.14 PSN-to-PSN communication at the data link layer.

protocol that exists at the host–PSN link may differ from that at the PSN–PSN link. The following procedures are involved.

The data link layer at the host A uses the message block or packet received from the layer above to construct a **frame** which will be passed to PSN A. This frame will then be transmitted to PSN B. If the subnet uses a different protocol then a different frame (containing the same message) will be constructed for the PSN–PSN transmission. The frame contains control information and the data message (see Figure 3.15).

A flag is used to indicate start and end of frame. This is a special bit pattern that cannot be used except for this purpose. However, techniques are available which permit the same bit sequence to occur as a valid part of the message. One efficient technique is **bit stuffing**. For example, if the flag is 01111110, then no sequence of six '1' bits is allowed, a '0' bit being inserted (stuffed) after every sequence of five '1' bits.

The **frame level control (FLC)** includes kind of frame, sequence number and acknowledgement indication. The kind of frame field allows the distinction between control frames (i.e. no data being transmitted) and data frames. The sequence field is used to identify frames within some time interval. It is possible for a frame to be considered lost when in fact it has suffered an unusually long delay. It will then be retransmitted and therefore both the original and the duplicate can reach the receiver. The sequence number helps to solve this problem. Since in this case both frames will have the same sequence number, one will be rejected. The acknowledgement field indicates on return to the sender that an error-free frame has been received by the destination node.

The **CRC (FCS)** field contains the hardware-computed cyclic redundancy code or **frame check sequence** (sometimes called **frame checksum**). On receipt of the frame, the data stream is used to compute the CRC. If the computed checksum does not agree with the one received, the frame is discarded and no acknowledgement is returned.

Flag	Frame level control (FLC)	Data	CRC (FCS)	Flag

Figure 3.15 The format of a data link frame.

The CRC is a polynomial code obtained in the following manner. The bit string is treated as representative of a polynomial with each bit being a coefficient. If the string has n bits then the polynomial has the n terms, x^{n-1} to x^0. Therefore the string 10010011 represents the polynomial

$$1.x^7 + 0.x^6 + 0.x^5 + 1.x^4 + 0.x^3 + 0.x^2 + 1.x^1 + 1.x^0$$

i.e. $x^7 + x^4 + x^1 + 1$. To compute the FCS for the m-bit message, the corresponding m-term polynomial must be divided by some agreed **generator polynomial** using modulo-2 arithmetic. The remainder is the FCS and it is appended to the message.

These fields facilitate the provision of a **connection oriented service** or an **acknowledged connectionless service**. In a connection oriented service a connection must be set up between the transmitting and receiving hosts before any data are transferred. Setting up a connection is similar to the dial-up and pick-up receiver phase in telephone communications. In computer communications the transmitter sends a request-to-send message and awaits a ready-to-accept response from the receiver before sending data. Furthermore, in the connection oriented service, the data link layer uses frame numbering and acknowledgement to guarantee that all frames are received exactly once and in the right order.

In an acknowledged connectionless service no connection is established. The transmitter can proceed immediately to the transmit data phase. However, each frame sent is acknowledged so that the transmitter can monitor the delivery. Frames can be resent if they are not acknowledged within some time-out interval.

It may be desirable to provide merely an **unacknowledged connectionless service**. As the name implies, data are transferred without connection establishment and without the acknowledgement of the message frames. Such a service may be used when either:

(a) the physical layer provides a relatively negligible error rate; or
(b) the layers above the data link possess mechanisms for any recovery desirable; or
(c) the information being transferred can suffer some loss without any dire need to recover.

The data link layer operations may seem simple, but in a realistic situation there will be varying numbers of unrelated message blocks arriving from different hosts, thus making heavy demands on buffering and other management capabilities at the PSN.

3.2.3 The network layer

The network layer is responsible for host-to-host communications. At this layer, the host receives a packet of information from the layer above it, adds its protocol header to the packet and uses the data link layer to transmit it to the PSN. At that PSN, the network layer selects a route to another PSN, then uses the data link layer to handle the link transmission. This process is repeated across the network until the packet is delivered to the destination host. The protocol header information will depend on the type of service, i.e. **virtual call** to support a connection oriented service, or **datagram** which supports a connectionless service.

Virtual call and datagram

In the virtual call environment, a virtual circuit is established before the message is transmitted. This means that a particular route is set up and will be used to transmit all the data packets, in the right sequence, relating to the particular communication exercise. In the datagram service, the network transmits each packet as a separate unit by using the best possible route available at the time. It means that packets may arrive out of order and it is the responsibility of the receiver to reassemble them into the right sequence.

In virtual call, the packet needs a destination address only for setting up the connection. Subsequent to this, a logical channel number which was assigned at set-up time is used. In datagram, each packet must carry the explicit destination address.

Routing, flow control

The subnet will most certainly have a number of possible physical paths between two hosts. Therefore there is the need to choose the best route to transmit packets. This means employing routing algorithms of which there are many alternatives. This routing characteristic is peculiar to the wide area point-to-point networks. That is, the packets travel from one point to a sole destination. There is the absence of the **broadcast** capability where packets 'in flight' can be captured by all nodes. Other concerns are *flow control* and *congestion*. The network must not be flooded with packets to the extent that there is a severe degradation of system performance levels.

3.2.4 The transport layer

This layer handles comunication between individual processes at different hosts. A user operates within a process environment. Therefore, communication between users involves communication between processes. The transport layer is designed to support such interprocess communication. The protocols in this layer are therefore implemented only at hosts and not in the PSNs.

A network-wide addressing scheme, which uniquely identifies not only all the processes offering some kind of service to the users of the network but also the valid user processes requesting any of those services, is fundamental to this transport service. The 'name servers' will usually provide this service.

The transport layer can support connection oriented or connectionless service. Before data transfer between processes begins in the connection oriented service, the sender process must request that a connection be established with the receiving process. On receipt by the sender of the 'connection accepted' indication from the receiving process, data transmission can commence. An explicit 'termination of connection' protocol ends the transmission. As was discussed under the lower layers, the connectionless service does not employ connection establishment and disconnection phases.

The level of error checking and other controls will be determined by the type of service provided by the lower layers. If a connection oriented service is required, and the network layer provides only a datagram service, there will be a great deal more work at the transport layer in order to ensure the level of integrity in the delivery of messages that is associated with a connection oriented service.

Many connections from one host to the same server process may be open at the same time. The receiving process may not be able to cope fast enough with all the incoming messages. In order to prevent the flooding of the receiver by fast incoming messages, buffering techniques and other flow control schemes must be employed.

3.2.5 The session layer

As we approach the topmost layer of the hierarchy, the issues addressed take on a strong application-oriented flavour. The session layer is the environment in which we see a departure from skeletal communication issues to the provision of user-oriented services. The user interacts with the network in order to obtain certain services. These user services are made available via sessions which have identifiable begin and end points and which must be carefully managed.

The management of a session involves the management of all the subtasks which are required to provide the service to the user. These subtasks may be mapped onto a number of different processes, one or more of which may be at a remote host. The session layer handles the interprocess communication between pairs of processes. This communication may at times be between only processes at the local host, whereas at other times it may be between a local host and remote host.

Therefore there exists a physical and logical separation between the session and transport layers. All local–remote communication is mapped onto the transport service. In a connection oriented service the session layer will use the transport layer to establish the connection with the remote host. However, the session may not have a one-to-one mapping with the transport connection. Indeed the session may require a series of transport connections and in some instances multiple sessions may be run in sequence over a single transport connection.

When there is a long task to be performed, e.g. the transfer of a large file, it would be disastrous if a failure near the completion of the task necessitated a restart of the entire task. In order to avoid this, the session layer divides these tasks into subtasks and ensures that there is no repeat of completed subtasks. In doing this, there is an attempt to make failures below this layer transparent to higher layers.

3.2.6 The presentation layer

The major concerns at this layer are:

(a) to ensure that information remains semantically sound when transmitted to a remote host that uses different data storage forms (e.g. different character codes and word lengths); and

(b) to provide an acceptable level of security and privacy to users of the network.

In short, the presentation layer handles the form in which data are presented to the network by the user, and delivered to the user by the network.

To achieve (a), there must be conversion, when necessary, of the data format used at a local host to the format used in the subnet for transmission through the net, followed by a conversion to the format used at the remote host before delivery.

To achieve (b), the raw data are converted into some coded form before transmission through the net and this is followed by a decode operation at the destination host. The security of this system will depend on how difficult it is for an intruder to break the code. This is an area of serious concern because of the highly confidential nature of information that may be transmitted through the network.

Several cryptographic techniques have been employed but the **encryption** method, which involves the use of secret keys, seems most favourable (see Section 4.5). In this method the raw or **plaintext** is transformed by an algorithm which is driven by a *key* (a bit string usually known only by the sender and receiver). The output from this transformation, called the **ciphertext**, is transmitted and on arrival the recipient uses the key to **decrypt** the ciphertext back into plaintext.

Additional security can be introduced by having two keys for each communication. An encode or 'E' key can be used to convert the plaintext to ciphertext, and a separate key – the decode or 'D' key – can be used to convert the ciphertext back into plaintext. With such a system, a user can distribute his encode key to all from whom he expects coded information, and he keeps his decode key secret, thus ensuring that he is the only one who can understand the text. The encode key is called a public key, hence such encryption systems are called 'public key cryptographic systems'.

3.2.7 The application layer

This, the highest layer in the hierarchy, is the one with which the user interacts. To the user, the network provides several services. These services are designed to meet the users' application needs. These applications vary with users but some general common interests can be identified. These have been dealt with in Chapters 1 and 2.

3.2.8 TCP/IP

TCP/IP, as indicated earlier, was developed by the ARPANET/Internet communities, and it has established a very good track record in terms of meeting most of the computer-to-computer communication needs. One of its main objectives was to provide effective communication across multiple, heterogeneous networks. In functionality, TCP is equivalent to the ISO/OSI transport layer, and IP is equivalent to the ISO/OSI network layer.

TCP/IP allows the running application to interact directly with the transport layer, thus removing the ISO/OSI presentation and session layers. The IP layer can run on any appropriately configured data link layer. Hence, the TCP/IP architecture admits the hierarchy denoted in Figure 3.16 (see Tanenbaum, 1996).

In Chapter 1 we made reference to many application-layer services which run on TCP. TCP actually refers to only one of the two types of service provided at the TCP/IP transport layer. TCP is the connection oriented service. The other service is connectionless, and is called the **UDP (User Datagram Protocol)** service (see Sections 3.2.2 to 3.2.4).

IP provides a datagram service (as discussed in Section 3.2.3) and attends to the routing, flow control and congestion issues pertinent to effective packet transmission across the inter-networks.

3.2.9 Local Area Networks

The Local Area Network (LAN) has a limited physical range and possesses some standard topology: bus, ring, star, etc. Due to these controlled features, many of

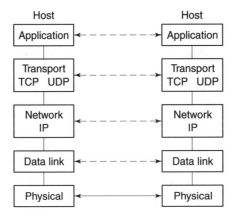

Figure 3.16 The TCP/IP five-layer protocol model.

the heavy protocol specifications are unnecessary. However, there still remains the need for standards to facilitate maintenance, scalability and interoperability. In widespread use are the **Institute of Electrical and Electronics Engineers (IEEE 802)** standardized Ethernet, Token-Ring and Fiber Distributed Data Interface (FDDI). These standards address essentially physical and data link layer concerns. Upon these layers, TCP/IP and several proprietary transport and user layer suites have been implemented.

3.2.10 Other technologies

New technologies are emerging constantly and the commonly used protocols are in many cases being stretched almost beyond the limit. At the same time there is serious activity in the area of new protocol specifications. Two technologies that are being given a great deal of attention are *ATM* and *Wireless Computing*.

ATM (Asynchronous Transfer Mode) is a technology that breaks up data into 53-byte packets, called cells, and transmits these cells from place to place through the network via a series of ultra-fast hardware switches. As in packet switching, different cells from the same message can take different routes across the network. ATM speeds begin at 155 Mbps, and the first-generation switches can run at 2.4 Gbps.

Wireless computing promises mobile users access to information anywhere and at any time. It allows users with a portable computer, often called a personal digital assistant or a personal communicator, to have a wireless connection to information networks. The more dominant applications being supported are mail-enabled applications and information services. In mail-enabled applications the users carrying personal communicators are able to receive and send electronic mail. Information services can provide access to popular database and bulletin-board type applications.

3.3 Summary

Many distributed systems are designed for long life. That life could be a miserable one for those who have to manage and maintain the system if the system's architecture is poor. It is good practice to ensure that there is sound technical judgment in the choice of software and hardware architecture.

Several models of architecture for distributed systems have emerged. From these models can be chosen a design that fits best the specific application and environment that are under study. We have discussed software architecture and network architecture.

The global software structures used include cooperating processes, process groups and client–server. In cooperating processes, processes interact with each other in order to perform some shared task. All the processes involved are not necessarily aware of all the interactions. In a process group message delivery always includes all the members of the group. In a client–server architecture the system is divided clearly between service consumers (the clients) and service providers (the servers).

The global structure can be viewed as a number of components neatly strung together. Attention must be paid to the structure of these components. Component design usually involves either a procedure-oriented model or an object-oriented model. The procedure-oriented approach sees the system as a number of steps to be performed on data entities. The object-oriented approach sees the system as a set of interrelated entities which possess state (data fields) and behaviour (methods).

The network architecture includes a number of protocol layers. The ISO/OSI seven-layer protocol reference model comprises a comprehensive set of specifications. Good functionality can be obtained in many environments with less heavyweight protocol suites. The Internet's TCP/IP protocol model enjoys very widespread acceptance. There are several other protocol architectures. The IEEE 802 set addresses primarily the local area network.

3.4 Questions

1 Indicate the key characteristics of the following distributed system structures:
  (a) cooperating processes
  (b) process groups
  (c) client–server.
2 How is inter-process activity synchronized in
  (a) Ada?
  (b) CSP?
  (c) Occam?
3 What is atomic broadcast in a message delivery system?
4 Distinguish between the three-message protocol and the single-shot protocol in client–server communication.
5 Distinguish between the procedure-oriented approach and the object-oriented approach to software design.
6 What is the function of the Java Virtual Machine?
7 What is CORBA?
8 What distributed system structure does CORBA support?
9 What is the role of the IDL in CORBA?
10 Give a rationale for a layered approach to a network architecture.
11 Name the seven layers in the ISO/OSI Reference Model.
12 How does TCP/IP differ from ISO/OSI?
13 Briefly indicate the major issues at each of the layers of the ISO/OSI Reference Model.
14 What is modulation? Describe three modulation techniques.

15 Compare and contrast the following transmission media:
   (a) twisted pair and coaxial cable
   (b) coaxial cable and optical fibers
   (c) terrestrial links and satellite.

16 Distinguish between time division multiplexing and frequency division multiplexing. Suggest any advantages that you think one technique has over the other.

17 Why is the packet switching technique more suitable than circuit switching for computer communications?

18 Distinguish between the virtual call and the datagram service at the network layer. Indicate any advantages that each enjoys over the other.

19 What differences are there between a wide area network and a local area network?

20 Indicate the significant features of the following technologies:
   (a) ATM
   (b) wireless computing.

21 Refer to the Student Registration system in Question 12 of Chapter 2. What global software structure should be adopted? What network architecture and topology would you recommend?

CHAPTER 4

Managing distributed resources

Distributed systems provide a wide array of services ranging from the simple messaging service to the hard real-time facility. We have discussed these in Chapter 1. These services can be set within specific distributed system areas which, quite wisely, must be constructed in accordance with solid architectural guidelines. Chapters 2 and 3 took us through these issues.

Many resources, large and small, hardware and software, some near and others far, are placed at the disposal of various target groups and individuals. Managing these resources well is integral to the successful running of the system. This issue of managing the resources will be looked at in this chapter under the following headings:

- Naming and addressing
- Sharing
- Availability and reliability
- Replication
- Privacy and security

4.1 Naming and addressing

The presence of the network increases the volume of names, and provides a distributed context in which the names can emerge and in which these names must be managed. The names are necessary to identify software, hardware, access privileges and the owners of all of these elements. Addressing should be independent of naming; however, the use of a name is most often linked to an attempt to locate something. Hence, addressing issues are closely associated with naming.

From the viewpoint of the user it is desirable if the name, while providing uniqueness, bears some descriptive character, e.g. master, account-file, since it is then easier to remember that name. This is immaterial from the system viewpoint where the objective might be to prevent easy guessing of a name, in which case a random string of bits might be the preferred name. Most systems tend to address both views.

For the uniqueness and description it is customary to use a multipart name, e.g.

node/group/user

where each part is associated with a particular level in a hierarchical naming structure. A good example of such names is the URL introduced in Section 1.2. In the case of a resource such as a file, this multipart name indicates the path through a hierarchical directory system to the file, e.g.

root-directory/sub-directory/filename

This pathname may denote a purely logical relationship with no specific physical address embedded in the name. Such a name is regarded as being *location independent*, and allows movement of the named entity without any change required to the name.

However, it will be necessary to have address mapping facilities easily available at some known location. In a distributed system, the use of such a name suggests a single global directory service such as is provided by some *file server* systems.

It might be desirable, at times, to have some level of address binding in the name, e.g.

node-NY/group/user

where node-NY identifies a specific location. This trades off some location independence for faster initial access, and is relatively efficient where interactions with an entity require a single access only.

In addition to the descriptive pathnames known by the user, the system can generate a secret, globally unique, bit-string name (usually called a **capability**) for a resource. This requires two levels of mapping: one from the symbolic user-known name to the capability, and the other from the capability to the location of the resource. In some cases the capability may possess a field which contains the address of the resource. We will discuss capabilities further in Section 4.2.

Whether the name is symbolic/descriptive or binary, a key concern in distributed systems is scalability. The naming system has to accommodate increasingly large numbers. One must envisage a time when a high percentage of the world's population may have to be electronically identified. It is therefore necessary that the name spaces – the collection of all valid names in the system – be chosen carefully.

The multipart scheme is one area in which this issue is addressed. Another area is the length of the data field for the individual part or component. A short field limits the size of the name space and is easier to forge. A long field provides a large name space but could be considered cumbersome to store and manipulate. It is often the practice to use a combination of long and short fields in multipart names.

4.1.1 Name servers

A general location-independent naming scheme incorporating users, services and resources can be supported by allocating the address translation responsibilities to a **name server**. Users can then use symbolic names with which they interact with the client machines. The clients then communicate with a name server which does the name to address resolution (see Figure 4.1).

The name server maintains look-up information to perform the translation from names to addresses. It is necessary that clients know the address only of the name server which will perform the name-to-address transformation. The request for the address of the resource/service is made only to initiate a session with the owner/server. Subsequent accesses to that owner/server within that session would not require interaction with the name server.

In addition, the name server may be designed to answer requests for the name of a resource/service given its address. This is particularly useful for monitoring purposes. Any alterations to the names of resources/services should be requested only by the nodes that own the resource or provide the service.

The performance of the network is, however, tied to the name server. Special measures must be taken to ensure the reliability of the name server. Table entries for critical resources may be held in non-volatile primary store to facilitate fast recovery after power failures. The hardware components should be robust and spares readily available to make the system acceptably resilient.

Furthermore, an arrangement can be made where clients can hold the addresses obtained from the name server on a long-term basis. This is suitable in a situation where clients make frequent accesses to certain resources whose addresses are not expected to change in the short term. Whenever there is a change in name-to-address mapping the name server can broadcast a short message indicating to clients that they must make the necessary update.

The implementation of the name server as a number of cooperating name servers distributed over the network can provide better performance than the

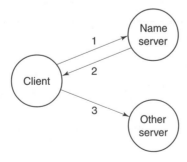

Figure 4.1 Client sends a request at 1 to the name server to obtain address of other server. The name server responds at 2 with requested address which client uses at 3 to contact other server.

single-server implementation. The name service database could be fully replicated, allowing clients to get service from the first reachable server.

On the other hand, the name service could be partitioned with each name server responsible for a specific region or domain. The domain name can then be incorporated into the multipart naming scheme.

4.1.2 Domain Name System

The Internet **Domain Name System (DNS)** is a distributed name service which employs partitioning, replication and caching to provide a relatively efficient naming system across the Internet (see Section 1.2). The naming system follows the hierarchical pattern discussed above. The tree structure is implemented as a multi-level set of domains (see Figure 1.4).

For example, cs.ucl.ac.uk and centre.uwi.tt are valid domain names in DNS. The highest level domain is on the right. Therefore centre.uwi.tt indicates that the domain centre.uwi.tt is in the domain uwi.tt (University of the West Indies, Trinidad & Tobago) which is in the domain tt (Trinidad & Tobago). The names within any domain are managed by that domain.

The DNS name service is primarily for resolving names into computer addresses or host names in the electronic mail and file transfer systems. The address returned by DNS is the IP address (Internet Protocol address: see Section 3.2) of a host computer on the Internet. No two computers can have the same IP address at the same time. The IP addresses most commonly used are IPv4. These are 32 bits long with the three fields – class, network number, host number – as depicted in Figure 4.2. It is customary to write the IP address as a four-part dotted string of decimal numbers with each part corresponding to a byte in the IP address. Therefore, the written addresses would range from 0.0.0.0 to 255.255.255.255.

8 bits	8 bits	8 bits	8 bits

Class A

0	Network	Host	

Class B

10	Network	Host	

Class C

110	Network		Host

Class D

1110	Multicast address		

Class E

11110	Reserved for future use		

Figure 4.2 IPv4 address formats.

At present it is impossible, using IPv4, to give every device on the Internet a globally unique IP address. The Internet has outgrown IPv4. Several clever temporary schemes (like rotating addresses among computers) are being employed. In order to correct this IPv6 has been specified. The address size has been expanded from the 32 bits of IPv4 to 128 bits in IPv6. However, due to the heavily installed base of IPv4 infrastructure, a slow transition to IPv6 is expected.

The DNS database is partitioned and replicated over a logical network of name servers. Name servers hold the part of the naming database pertinent to its local domain, as well as domain names and addresses of other name servers to which names that cannot be resolved in the local domain must be passed.

4.1.3 Directory service

A name service can have more features than merely the name to address translation capability. Other attributes (type of computer, size of memory) of the named entity can be stored; and there might be the facility to access entities by supplying attribute values. The name service can be incorporated into a more comprehensive *directory service* which allows not only the locating of services and resources, but also the supplying of information on people.

X.500 is a good example of such a directory service. It was defined by CCITT and ISO as a service for access to information about 'real-world entities'. X.500 provides both the telephone-like 'white-page' access and 'yellow-page' access. In X.500 entities are represented as named nodes in a tree structure.

Each node has a range of attributes. The name of a node is used for 'white-page' access, and attributes are used for 'yellow-page' access. An X.500 name is a list of *attribute=value* items separated by commas. Attributes are denoted by a standard code, e.g. C is country, O is organization, OU is organization unit, TITLE is title, and SURNAME is, of course, surname. These can be used thus:

```
/C=GB/O=UCL/OU=CS/TITLE=DR/SURNAME=WHIZ/
```

to identify Dr Whiz at the Computer Science department at UCL in the UK. The slashes are used to indicate the path through the tree structure.

4.2 Sharing

Sharing is a key attribute of distributed systems. Naming and addressing allow users and resources to be uniquely identified and located. Sharing brings users and resources together in order to achieve acceptable outcomes. Before a resource can be allocated to a user, that user must be required to demonstrate to the system that he or she possesses some right of access. That is, the user must be subjected to an authentication procedure.

ACL for Resource0

Staff	RE
System	RWE
Student	R

Figure 4.3 An Access Control List showing mixes of R (read), W (write)
and E (execute) for three classes of users.

One approach is to require that the user supply a name (ID) and a password.
These are checked against stored lists for validity following which the access
requests are checked out against some **Access Control List** (ACL). An ACL is a
per-resource list which indicates who the valid users of the resource are and what
are the rights of access that these users enjoy. It is customary to categorize users
into classes (also called protection domains) where all the members of a given
class possess the same access rights. Figure 4.3 shows an ACL with three classes
enjoying different mixes of read, write and execute rights.

An unauthorized user can beat this system by masquerading as a valid user (i.e.
a valid member of a class). The inter-networks offer a vast unsupervised space for
possible masqueraders. Hence some more control is necessary. A Capability List
(CL) could be used. In a capability-based system access rights are embedded in a
relatively long, system-generated bit string called a capability, which cannot be
easily guessed.

The system will then maintain a per-user CL of capabilities, one capability for
each resource to be accessed; and a per-resource CL of capabilities, one for each
protection domain or class of user. Whenever a user attempts to access a resource,
the system will retrieve from that user's CL the associated capability. Before
access is permitted this capability must match with a capability in the CL of the
resource (see Figure 4.4).

The behaviour here is therefore analogous to that of presenting a ticket
(a capability) which must be validated before access is allowed. If an intruder
can obtain a valid ticket or forge one then the system can be compromised. In
Section 4.5 we shall examine additional security measures that can be employed.

System Class CL

Resource0	Capability with RWE
Resource1	Capability with RE
Resource2	Capability with E

Resource0 CL

Capability with RWE
Capability with RE
Capability with E

Figure 4.4 A capability list CL for a user in System class. The capability presented
by a user must match with that in a resource CL, e.g. system class users can
Read, Write and Execute Resource0.

When sharing a resource among a number of users the issues of scheduling and allocation will arise. In considering scheduling and allocation, we can distinguish between two cases:

(a)   the resource belongs to a pool of identical resources; or
(b)   there is only one instance of the resource.

In the case where the resource is one of a pool, state information can be held centrally on the members of the pool. Any available member can be allocated to a requesting user based on a first-come, first-served discipline or a priority scheme that involves some characteristic of the user. One has to be careful when using a priority scheme to ensure that **indefinite postponement** (also called starvation) does not occur. Indefinite postponement can arise when a waiting user (process, task) always has to give way to a higher priority user.

The system objectives will determine the scheme, and it is sometimes necessary to strike a comfortable balance between conflicting objectives. For example, minimizing the communication cost can be at odds with reducing response times in transaction processing.

In order to minimize communication cost, it will be necessary always to try to allocate local resources or those nearest to the requesting site. On the other hand, a reduction in the response time may only be possible by increasing the level of distribution.

These concerns may be adequate for a hardware pool such as a pool of processors, but if the resource belongs to a software pool, e.g. several copies of a file, replicated system tables, or a distributed database, particular attention has to be paid to the preservation of the overall consistency of the stored information.

The resource may be a single object, e.g. a single copy of a file, or a special purpose processor. Multiple readers can be permitted to the file, but a writer should be allowed exclusive access. If the file can be divided into several parts (pages) and concurrent access permitted to these distinct parts, then scheduling and allocation become more complex (see Chapter 5).

4.2.1 Sharing primary memory

A special aspect of resource sharing is the sharing of primary memory. During runtime a program (process) executes in its address space. The address space is the extent of primary memory that the program is authorized to access. In a single-computer system without virtual memory, a memory protection scheme (e.g. base and bounds registers, protection keys) limits concurrent processes to their address spaces within the shareable primary memory. Processes can share variables and procedures (i.e. allow address spaces to intersect) by establishing critical sections with the necessary concurrency control features. This is an integral part of your Operating Systems design course.

In a single-computer system with virtual memory, executing processes have an address space of virtual memory which at runtime is incrementally mapped onto primary memory. This mapping involves the transparent transfer of pages from disk and update of page tables. Other issues such as page removal and the write-back of pages to disk are all critical to this design. Critical section management will be necessary when address spaces intersect.

In a distributed system, where a network of computers is involved, it is quite useful to have a programming model where the address space of the program is distributed in a transparent way across the memories of many computers. This is the **distributed shared memory (DSM)** model of distributed computing. Many perceive the day, sometime soon, when a program's address space crisscrosses the Internet.

We saw in Chapter 3 how the processes in a distributed system interact with each other across the network via remote procedure call and message passing. In this model a process owns its local address space and explicitly packages some data to be passed to another process which also executes in its local address space. This is not the DSM model.

A simple, though inefficient, DSM scheme can extend the virtual memory model to include remote memories with dynamic mapping and transfer at runtime. Alternatively, it is felt that new architectures such as the Object Request Broker, JavaBeans and Components may provide the environment for effective DSM. Distributed shared memory will be looked at in some detail in Chapter 6.

4.3 Availability and reliability

Availability and reliability are issues of performance. A system is considered to be performing well if it produces satisfactory service outcomes. The system may at times produce incorrect outcomes and at other times produce no outcome at all, i.e. it fails to deliver service. A system that does not produce an outcome is for that period of time unavailable. This is often due to some component failure.

However, if there was no failure and eventually there was a service outcome, but too late to be of any use, then relative to that service request the system was unavailable. If you were waiting on the 8.30 a.m. bus to get to your 9.00 a.m. appointment, a 20-minute journey away, you would certainly not consider the service as being available if the bus showed up at 9.00 a.m.

Availability is regarded as a measure of the ability of the system to deliver service correctly whenever there is a demand. Reliability is a measure of the correctness with which the system delivers. The correctness of information addresses primarily the issues of detecting and correcting errors that have occurred in stored and/or transmitted data. Some of this we have already discussed in Sections 3.2.1 and 3.2.2.

Fundamental to receiving the service is being able to reach the service provider and/or the resource easily and quickly. Being reachable is first of all a computer network issue. An adequate communication channel must exist between user and resource. It would not be very sensible to install a distributed system on a network that cannot accommodate the normal workload traffic. There would be a major availability crisis.

4.3.1 Local Area Networks

If the system is for a LAN installation, then one must determine whether the information-carrying capacity on the LAN can handle the traffic. Rough estimates can be obtained by counting the number of nodes on the network, the number of messages each node transmits in some unit time (during normal workload, during peak time), and the average length of a message, and by matching these against the quoted transmission rate of the LAN and the delays that arise from the channel access methods (e.g. collision detection time and token holding time).

Of concern too in a LAN is how vulnerable the system is to a single point of failure. For example, a station on a ring LAN fails to propagate the token, or a bridge between two bus segments fails, thus partitioning the network, or some other physical component malfunctions. These are all availability and reliability issues which can impact on the distributed system. However, they are best addressed in a Local Area Networks course (see Naugle, 1991).

4.3.2 Wide Area Networks

The distributed system may be running over a Wide Area Network (WAN) or inter-networks (e.g. accessible via the Internet). There are many network factors here that can affect availability and reliability. Some of these are as follows:

(a) The number of possible routes through the network between user and resource. If one route is unavailable can another one be found?
(b) The channel capacity through the various communication links. Feeding a low capacity link off a much higher capacity link can create congestion, loss of messages, many retransmissions and other unpleasant results. Furthermore, in many cases, there may be adequate capacity for text data, but inadequate capacity for multimedia.
(c) The communication protocols employed. For example, a flow control protocol in a network could slow the traffic down to a point below the quality of service expected in the distributed system.

These network issues are best handled in a course on computer networks (see Tanenbaum, 1996).

It is seen that the network channels can affect availability and reliability, but so too can the computing nodes. The capacity on the channels could be more than adequate but the nodes could be found wanting. For example, a server might be too slow to handle a large percentage of the requests it receives. There are both hardware and software strategies that can be employed in addressing this problem. The hardware approach usually involves processor and memory upgrades, while under software better algorithms, data storage and information retrieval techniques are adopted.

4.3.3 Processor and memory upgrades

Increased processor power helps availability. So too do increased primary memory and faster-access secondary memory. Memory caches are often employed to reduce the number of accesses to lower-level memories or the number of requests to some server (e.g. caching in a name service). This alleviates the contention for shared single resources, improves throughput time and hence increases availability.

A cache is a high speed memory module which is connected to a processor for its private use and which maintains copies of actively referenced material. The maintaining of a cache is feasible due to the locality principle that operates in computation. This locality principle exhibits both **temporal locality** and **spatial locality** characteristics.

In **temporal locality** the same memory location is referenced repeatedly within a small interval of time. In **spatial locality** neighbouring memory locations are referenced within a small interval of time.

In distributed systems one of the prime objectives is the exploiting of inherent parallelism in the computational tasks so as to obtain better throughput times. This can mean different processes executing in separate processors on shared data. In a cached system this can require the existence of multiple copies of the same information distributed over the private caches. Furthermore, processes can migrate to other processors with the associated generation of multiple copies of the same information across separate caches.

This copying presents a problem. Each processor can alter its private cache. Therefore, what is the state of the copies in the other caches? What is the state of the global memory from which the cached copies were obtained originally? This problem is referred to as the **cache coherence** or **cache consistency** problem. Software and hardware solutions have been implemented to deal with this problem.

Software techniques involve the marking of memory areas in order to indicate, first of all, what is shared data as opposed to non-shared data. Non-shared data can be classified as cacheable; so too can read-only shared data. Shared read–write data can be classified as always non-cacheable or as non-cacheable by all except one process during execution phases. During such an execution phase, exclusive access by a single process is allowed. Any updates to the cached variables must be recorded in main memory. This update to main memory can be done by using either a *write-through* or a *copy-back* update policy.

In the write-through policy all updates to the cache are immediately written to the main memory. In the copy-back policy the cache is flushed at the end of the referencing interval by rewriting it to main memory.

Hardware techniques employ either the *write-invalidate* or the *write-update* principle. The write-invalidate principle invalidates all the other cache copies of data whenever there is an update to one cache copy. In this scheme the altered copy is then the only copy available for accessing. The write-update policy maintains consistency by immediately propagating all updates to the other cache copies. The updating time of the main memory can vary with implementation.

These hardware policies are embedded in two hardware techniques: *snoopy cache protocols* and *directory schemes*. In a snoopy cache protocol all the caches process all the cache commands to determine whether the invalidate or update command refers to data in the cache. That is, the caches listen to or 'snoop on' all the commands. In the directory scheme a directory of copies is maintained to register the contents of all the caches. Cache invalidate or update commands can then be sent directly to the pertinent caches. Stenstrom (1990) provides an interesting survey of several cache coherence issues.

Secondary memory constitutes another area where availability can be improved. In particular the aim is to provide faster access to the stored data. A useful approach is to organize the storage in order to facilitate as much parallel access as possible. Effective techniques that have been employed include storing copies of data on multiple disk drives or installing RAID (redundant array of inexpensive disks) systems.

RAID technology uses disk **striping** to improve availability. In striping, the data to be stored is spread across a number of disks. If a file is spread over n disks then, in theory, n users could be allowed simultaneous access to a mutually exclusive nth part of that file. However, in real terms it depends on, among other things, the size of receiving buffers and the type of striping. Disk striping schemes include fine-grained striping and coarse-grained striping.

Fine-grained striping is bit- or byte-level striping where each disk contains a bit or byte of every block of data. In this arrangement the retrieval of a block involves accessing all the disks simultaneously. In coarse-grained striping each disk holds a block of the file and requests are serviced by accessing each disk in succession. RAID technology is particularly suitable for accommodating multiple user accesses to single, large files such as in video server systems (see Section 2.4).

4.3.4 Software design

In programming terms, access to the resource is via a process or server (i.e. some software module) running at a node in the network. The user requests from across the network arrive at this server via a communication port on the server node (see Figure 4.5). If this node is a uniprocessor computer, then every arriving request will normally generate an interrupt and cause a suspension of any other processing activity. Since the CPU may be faster than the communication

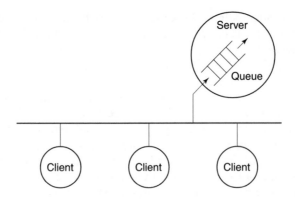

Figure 4.5 Client requests join the queue at Server.

channel, then irrespective of the rate of incoming requests, given that there is unlimited buffer space, it is possible that the server could accept (not necessarily process) all the requests.

This is analogous to a solo concert performer who, in addition to singing, must also handle the ushering of the patrons. If there is a constant stream of arrivals, whom the performer must show to a seat, then there will certainly not be much singing. A situation like this where the computing power is inordinately consumed by interrupt processing is described as **livelock**. A hardware solution might involve deploying more functional capability. However, good design dictates that software strategies are also relevant.

A fundamental design issue here is the ease with which switching from the handling of one request to the handling of another can be done. It is necessary to remove as much of the processing overhead as is possible. For example, assume a simple file server that handles 'read file(page no.)' and 'write file(page no.)' requests from clients. The server can be coded as a software module that includes the procedures:

Procedure 0: *Seek file*(page no.)
{this locates the page on disk via directory system}

Procedure 1: *Read file*(page no.)
{this returns the page to client}

Procedure 2: *Write file*(page no.)
{this writes a page to disk}

It should be very easy for you to deduce that, in theory, several requests could be handled concurrently by this server. However, whether or not this is achieved in practice depends on how the software is implemented. If the three procedures are bundled as one process with a single path of execution, then the normal process behaviour would force serial execution of requests.

This occurs because the OS (operating system) would view the process as the smallest executable entity to which the processor is allocated, and the OS would block the process on every disk event. That is, if any one of procedures 0, 1 or 2 is being executed, no other procedure will be allowed to run.

An alternative implementation is to construct the procedures as separate processes. In this arrangement the procedures are viewed as independent processes by the OS and are therefore allowed to run concurrently. When one process is blocked on a disk event, another process can be dispatched. The management of the concurrency is, of course, a critical matter which we shall discuss in Chapter 5. Since the processes are treated independently by the OS, the blocking and dispatching are heavyweight functions generating much overhead. This is the context-switch overhead which includes saving of state, register and other information on behalf of the blocked process, and loading from corresponding save-areas on behalf of the dispatched process. This does not help the cause of availability.

Hence the use of the multi-threaded approach introduced in Section 2.5. If the software environment permits it (and in distributed systems one should ensure that the environment does) the three procedures can be expressed as separate threads within a single process. In this way, concurrent execution can be enjoyed without the heavyweight context switching.

As indicated in Section 3.1.4, Java supports multi-threaded programming. There is a class Thread in the Java class library. This facilitates creating, configuring, running and synchronizing the concurrent execution of threads, for example:

```
class SeekReq extends Thread {
   String filename;              // creates a Thread object

   SeekReq(String name) {        // initializes the Thread object
      filename = name;
   }

   public void run() {
                                 // this method will be executed
                                 // when the Thread runs
      return;
   }

   public static void main(String[] args) {
      new SeekReq('' '').start();    // the start method must be
                                 // invoked to spawn a new
                                 // thread of control before
                                 // thread runs
   }
}
```

Correspondingly, threads for the other procedures can be created. We shall examine the synchronizing of concurrent execution in Chapter 5.

We have seen already how the distribution of the processing functions across several computers can help availability. In particular, we saw in Section 2.5 how agent processes can be deployed across the network to represent the interests of a network operating system. Then there is the client–server architecture in Sections 2.1 and 3.1.3 which allow separation based on produce and consume functions.

4.3.5 Databases

Databases can be partitioned, allowing parts of the database to be 'closer' to where they are needed (see Section 2.2), or it may be necessary to access separately stored databases in order to satisfy some query. A desirable objective would be to provide a distributed service whose availability is not affected adversely by the partitioned data.

As an example, assume that International Auto-Rentals had its database to support auto rentals partitioned as in Figure 4.6 and the following request was received in London:

Make a reservation for Dorothy Swift on a red sports car to be picked up in New York on (date and time given), a small hatchback to be picked up by Jill Plain in Los Angeles on (date and time given) and a station wagon for Jack Baggage in London on (date and time given).

Since the objective is good database availability, it would be necessary to find the relevant relations (or objects) quickly. Full replication, which will be discussed in the next section, is one approach. A replicated dictionary with address mappings is required. Once the relations (objects) are located, a decision must be made quickly on what should be shipped. The customer could be expecting an immediate response.

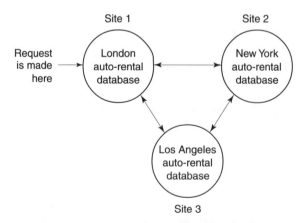

Figure 4.6 Auto-rental distributed database partitioned over three sites.

The request can be split into three queries: one each for New York, Los Angeles and London; and the remote queries shipped to the owner sites. The subquery processing is then done at the three sites and the responses returned to the initiator. Alternatively, the pertinent records or pages (from the relations or objects) could be shipped from the remote sites for processing at the initiator.

This latter approach may, at first thought, seem unwise since the updates will eventually have to be written back to the owner sites. However, there may be other information conveyed which can be cached for subsequent processing, and the write-back could be delayed to be done at a convenient low-traffic period.

When shipping requests or data across the network it is necessary too that consideration be given to CPU-load distribution, and what priority will be attached to incoming tasks. In this example the time differences across the three sites may also be a factor in determining how to process.

4.4 Replication

In Section 1.3 we highlighted the importance of replication in distributed systems. Maintaining copies of resources at separate nodes in the network can improve the pattern of communication traffic, help load sharing, reduce response times, and offer an alternative when a resource becomes unavailable. For these reasons replication is a key attribute of many distributed systems. We have seen already how replication is involved in the Domain Name System discussed in Section 4.1. However, replication is not free; the replicas must be managed to provide primarily a satisfactorily consistent image to all the users. In Section 3.1.2 we introduced the process group architecture as an effective approach for managing replicas.

4.4.1 Replicas as members of a group

Identifying and reaching the replicas are primary concerns. Within the group architecture these are membership issues. These must be handled by a membership service. The membership service itself could be provided by a single server or it could be distributed across the nodes as a number of cooperating processes (see Section 3.1.1).

The membership service would allow, at least, the following commands:

```
CreateGroup
JoinGroup
LeaveGroup
```

In response to the CreateGroup command a unique group identifier is returned and a membership list is initialized. It is usual for this command to be invoked by (or on behalf of) a process which now becomes the first member on the list. The list maintains a unique process identifier and an address (or some facility to obtain the address).

The `JoinGroup` command requests that the calling process or a process identified by its unique process ID be included in the group identified.

The `LeaveGroup` command allows the calling process or an identified process to leave the identified group. A member may leave the group voluntarily or through failure. If a member fails (or cannot be reached) then this will have been detected (or assumed) by the membership service or by a member and an appropriate `LeaveGroup` command issued.

A new member joining or a member leaving changes the composition of the group. This is a significant event in which some if not all active members might be interested. For example, if the membership changes during the multicast of a message how should the outcome of the multicast be classified? What if the replicas were participating in transaction processing and a member failed – what happens next? What if the failed member were in fact the coordinator of the activity?

It is therefore necessary that group changes be known and that a group change be synchronized with other pertinent group activity. In the ISIS toolkit (introduced in Section 3.1.2) group changes are handled by the maintenance of group views. A view captures the current membership list and bears a unique identifier (i.e. a sequence number). A group view $view_{i+1}$ differs from its immediate predecessor $view_i$ either by the addition of a new member or by the departure of a member voluntarily or through failure.

Group activity, e.g. message passing, can then be associated with a particular view. Should the view change before an activity is complete, a decision can be made with respect to the outcome of that activity. It is therefore necessary that the view change be effectively coordinated. This is primarily a message delivery issue.

In Section 3.1.2 we highlighted some key issues pertinent to message delivery within a process group. Sending a message to all members of a group is known as **multicasting**. Muticasting can have different outcomes depending on the reliability guarantees and the ordering options that are available.

The usual reliability classes are

- unreliable multicast
- reliable multicast
- atomic multicast,

and the usual ordering classifications are

- unordered
- totally ordered
- causally ordered
- sync ordered.

4.4.2 Reliability of message delivery

In Sections 3.1.3 and 3.2.2 we discussed the need, at times, to monitor message delivery. The primary way in which this is done is by requiring that the receipt of error-free messages be acknowledged. This can be done explicitly or, if certain conditions are satisfied by the communicators, the bad messages can be negatively acknowledged rather than acknowledging the good ones. This can generate savings in communication cost since it can often be assumed that the ratio of corrupted to error-free messages is very small.

Indeed many strategies can be employed to reduce the cost of communication in message delivery systems. If the content of the message is of very little importance or there is great confidence in the communication infrastructure then the sender can choose unreliable multicast. In unreliable multicast an attempt is made to deliver the message to all the members of the group without acknowledgement. In practice, this involves transmitting the message once.

Reliable multicast uses a monitoring scheme to ensure that some (if not all) members of the group receive the message. Atomic multicast is a reliable multicast that guarantees that either all operational members in the group receive the message or none of them do.

Any member of the group can fail during the multicast. The essence of this atomic protocol is for the original to receive acknowledgements from all live members. If no acknowledgement is received after some time-out interval the message can be resent (up to some maximum number of times). After failing to hear within some time limit (or after the repeated resends) a member is deemed to have failed.

- What if the originator fails?
- How can this be determined?
- Should another member take over?
- Who should take over?

If the originator, who is monitoring the multicast, fails then it cannot be ascertained that the atomic multicast is complete. Therefore the originator must be monitored to determine failure. Since any member can fail then all the members of the group must monitor the originator. An effective way to do this is to require that the originator multicast an 'I'm alive' message periodically. This can be conveyed implicitly with another regular message or it can be explicit when there is no other message to send within the stipulated period.

On determining failure another member must assume the role of originator and attempt to complete the multicast. However, since more than one member can determine the failure, this presents the problem of which member should take over. This is in fact a common problem wherever there is a leader or coordinator in a group. Many solutions have been proposed. Since it involves generally an election of a leader, the solutions are categorized as **election algorithms**.

An election algorithm is invoked when a member of the group concludes that the leader has failed. That member can then attempt to take over the leadership. Since another member can attempt concurrently to assume leadership, the algorithm must provide a mechanism to resolve the conflict. A simple approach is to assign increasing member numbers and let the highest numbered member take over the leadership. This is sometimes referred to as the Bully Algorithm since the 'biggest bloke on the block' always wins.

In this algorithm a member, on deciding that the leader has failed, multicasts an 'I am prepared to take over' election message to higher numbered members. If no one responds, that member wins and multicasts an 'I am the new leader' message to all operational members. If a higher numbered member receives the election message, it responds with its own 'I am prepared to take over' message, whereupon the lower numbered member backs off.

4.4.3 Message ordering

You should recall the importance of message ordering and the need to distinguish between separate group views (see Section 3.1.2). Inconsistencies can arise if the appropriate message ordering is not enforced. We shall now discuss the different types of ordering that are listed above.

Unordered multicast

In unordered multicast no mechanism is provided to impose any order on message delivery. This option is chosen when the action or state generated by a message is commutative with another message or messages. For example, if messages m_1 and m_2 are read-only requests to a stable file, then the opposite orderings m_1m_2 and m_2m_1 will produce the same effect. It will therefore be unnecessary to request ordering, especially since ordering is relatively costly.

Totally ordered multicast

Totally ordered multicast ensures that all members of the group see (i.e. process) a given set of messages in the same order. Therefore any two messages m_1 and m_2 will be delivered everywhere either in the sequence m_1m_2 or as m_2m_1. Several applications may desire totally ordered multicast. One example is in the multicast of transactions which include a mix of debit and credit operations to a replicated account file.

Totally ordered multicast is relatively expensive. Fundamental to this option is the allocation of a sequence number to each message and the global ordering of the messages based on these sequence numbers. The main approaches used are

- centralized sequencing
- distributed sequencing
- clocks.

In centralized sequencing a single member, the *sequencer*, is responsible for allocating the sequence number to a message. Therefore, before a message can be delivered, a sequence number must be obtained from the sequencer. Lower numbered messages are processed before higher numbered ones. Members keep a record of the next sequence number expected (or the last one received) so that, should an out-of-order one arrive, it can be held back until the correct one in the sequence arrives. This adjustment can be achieved through negative acknowledgements (explicit or implicit) and retransmissions.

Since it is necessary to hold back messages that are out of sequence, a useful strategy is to build two queues for message ordering at each replica: the first queue, a *hold-back queue*, for arriving messages whose order has not been finalized, and the second queue, a *stable queue* (also called a processing or delivery queue), for those messages whose processing order has been finalized (see Figure 4.7).

Distributed sequencing achieves totally ordered multicast without a central sequencer. Members of the group participate, via an exchange of messages, in a message sequencing agreement protocol. It involves the suggestion of a number by the initiator of a multicast to the other members of the group, who then respond with their own suggestions. The initiator then uses the information received to make a final selection.

For example, in ISIS each member records F_{max}, the largest agreed final number, and P_{max}, its own largest proposed number. On receiving a message with a proposed number, each receiving member i responds to the initiator with its own proposed number computed as

$$\max(F_{max}, P_{max}) + 1 + i/n$$

where n is the number of members.

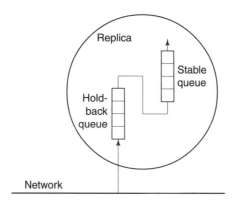

Figure 4.7 Incoming messages are held on hold-back queue where final ordering is established before a message is moved to stable queue for processing.

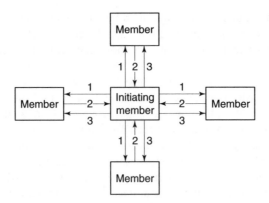

Figure 4.8 The initiating member sends a proposed number (message 1) to the other members. Each member sends its own proposed number at 2. The initiator makes a selection and informs all members in message 3.

Each member will place the message with its own proposed number on its hold-back queue. The initiator collects all the proposals from which it selects the largest number. All members are then notified of this final number, whereupon the correct ordering can be established (see Figure 4.8). The use of clocks will be discussed in Section 5.3.

Causally ordered multicast

Causal ordering is described as happened-before ordering. That is, there is a logical relationship between two events which establishes a single correct order in which these events must be performed. For example, to undress oneself follows dressing oneself, i.e. dress happened-before undress; posting an item on a bulletin board happened-before the response to that item. Causally ordered multicast ensures that if m_1 happened-before m_2 then m_1 is processed before m_2 at all members of the group.

An effective technique for implementing causally ordered multicast is the use of **vector timestamps**. Vector timestamps were originally referred to as version vectors with notable use in the LOCUS distributed operating system (Walker et al., 1983). The basic principle is to allow replicas to exist in different versions and ensure that these versions can be causally ordered.

Let the initial state of a replica be classified as version 0 and each message received increases the version number by 1; then after receiving three messages a replica would show version 3. However, since more than one member is involved, it is necessary that, for causal ordering, the version number reflect each member's contribution. Therefore, the version is expressed as a vector with an entry for the number of messages received from each member. For example, the timestamp (2, 4, 3, 1, 3) would indicate that there are five members in the group and the member holding this vector timestamp has received two messages from member 1, four from member 2, three from member 3 and so on. Two versions V_i and V_j are causally ordered if and only if each entry in V_i's vector timestamp is less than or equal to the corresponding entry in V_j's vector timestamp.

In order to support causally ordered multicast, the multicast message must carry a vector timestamp. This timestamp is provided by the initiating member, and is generated by incrementing by 1 its own entry position in the vector of the replica that it owns. For example, if the replica owned by member 3 has the vector timestamp (2, 4, 3, 1, 3) and initiates a multicast relating to this replica, then it would update its timestamp to (2, 4, 4, 1, 3) and this would be the timestamp carried by the multicast. Receiving members can use the arriving timestamps to establish causal order.

Sync-ordered multicast

Sync-ordering, as the name implies, is an attempt to put everything 'in-sync'. Therefore, in the context of message delivery, a sync-ordered message m divides messages received into two mutually exclusive sets at all members: a set 1 of messages received before m and a set 2 of messages received after m.

It is at this point that you can recall our discussion above on group changes and the critical need not only to inform the members of the change but also to synchronize group changes. It is to meet a need like this that the sync-ordered multicast is required. Group view changes can be multicast as a message to be sync-ordered with respect to other messages. In this way a clear dividing line can be drawn between some view $view_i$ and the following view $view_{i+1}$. The desired outcome relative to message delivery is that the multicast must be associated with a view. If the view-change sync-ordered message is multicast while another multicast m is current, then either m can be considered as failed and all its effects removed or m is delivered in the following view.

4.5 Privacy and security

Privacy and security are protection issues. The managing of distributed resources must include the task of protecting those resources from unauthorized users and from the negative effects of faulty or poorly designed system components. Failure in hardware and software and poor system design can compromise the security system. If a window in your bedroom falls out (a faulty system component) it affects your privacy and security. However, you do not normally expect your guard dog or your security officer to check for defects on your window, although you might be able to argue that it could be logically added to their duties.

The privacy and security issues in resource management address the structures and procedures that are established specifically to prevent unauthorized access to the resources. Although these structures and procedures tend to exist like an envelope around the basic system, their effectiveness can be reduced or even eliminated by faults on the inside. Therefore, while we discuss the envelope in this section, we cannot over-emphasize the need to ensure that the underlying structures are solid.

In Section 4.2 we looked at the sharing of resources. Mechanisms for permitting and restricting access to resources were discussed. These form an integral part of a security system for distributed resources. The measures discussed included names and passwords for authentication, and access control lists and capabilities for enforcing access privileges.

In a distributed system information flows through the communication networks which often traverse 'unfriendly' territory. It is therefore necessary, as an added security measure, to encode the messages via some secret formula. Indeed, such a coding procedure is not only useful for message passing but can be viewed as a last line of defence in the event that unauthorized access to stored data is obtained.

4.5.1 Cryptography

The science of sending secret messages is known as **cryptography**, and crypto-graphic systems are now in widespread use in distributed computing. These systems provide an authentication service and a secure message delivery service. The authentication service prevents the intruder from impersonating a valid user, and secure message delivery offers the guarantee that should a message fall into the hands of the wrong person that message cannot be interpreted.

The basic constituent elements of a cryptographic system (see Figure 4.9) are:

- the *plaintext*, which is the information material that is to be coded;
- the *ciphertext*, which is the coded information;
- the *encryption algorithm*, which is the method used for encoding;
- the *decryption algorithm*, which is the method used for decoding;
- the *key*, which is a parameter used as input with the plaintext or ciphertext to encode or decode respectively; and
- the *principals*, which are those on whose behalf the security system is working.

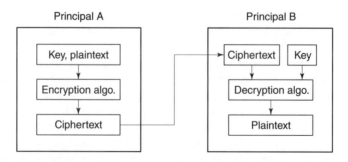

Figure 4.9 Block diagram of cryptographic message transfer from A to B.

Cryptographic systems have been classified as **secret key** cryptographic systems or as **public key** cryptographic systems. In secret key cryptography the same key, which must be kept secret among the principals, is used for both the encode and the decode functions. In public key cryptography the encode key differs from the decode key. The decode key is kept secret by the receiving principal while the encode key is made public for all possible senders.

4.5.2 Secret key cryptography

The Data Encryption Standard (**DES**) is a widely used secret key cryptographic system. In DES the encryption algorithm encrypts data in 64-bit blocks. A 56-bit key is used as a parameter to perform a sequence of bit rotations and transpositions on the 64-bit blocks of plaintext. The decryption algorithm uses the same 56-bit key and runs the reverse sequence on the 64-bit blocks of ciphertext. The algorithm is in the public domain but the keys, which are very difficult to forge, must be kept secret.

Finding a correct key (i.e. breaking the system) is essentially a trial-and-error task. It involves obtaining blocks of associated plaintext and ciphertext pairs and systematically trying a number of fabricated keys until the correct one is found. The longer the key the harder is this exercise. However, with the right skill, a great deal of time and a lot of computing power, the system can be broken.

Although the level of security provided by DES is satisfactory to many applications, there has been some concern over the 56-bit key length. It is felt that, in other areas, the greater security afforded by longer keys is preferred. One important example of secret key encryption with a longer key is the International Data Encryption Algorithm (**IDEA**). IDEA also takes 64-bit blocks of plaintext through a sequence of parametrized transformations, but unlike DES it uses a 128-bit key.

Secret key distribution

The cryptographic system will be ineffective if the keys are not kept secret among the principals. The keys must be distributed in a secure way such that only authentic principals would possess the secret key. Secure secret key distribution has been based on the Needham and Schroeder secret key authentication protocol. A derivative of this protocol is given in Figure 4.10.

A trusted third party is used to manage the key distribution. This trusted third party is called the *authentication server*. The authentication server provides a secure way for pairs of principals to obtain keys. Each principal is registered with the authentication server S who provides the principal with a secret key that is used only for communication with S. For example, principals A and B use secret keys K_A and K_B respectively to communicate with S. A message M encrypted with a key K is expressed as $K\{M\}$.

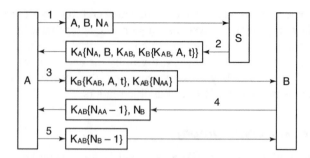

Figure 4.10 Secret key authentication using a protocol derived
from Needham–Schroeder.

The protocol allows principal A to initiate secure communication with principal B. A sends a message to S requesting a secret key to be used for secure communication with B. This message is uniquely identified by a nonce (N_A) so as to avoid its replay by an intruder who might have captured the original. A nonce can be chosen from a sequence of integers or it can be a timestamp, so long as it is sufficient to establish the freshness of a message.

S responds to A in a message encrypted in A's secret key K_A. This message contains the nonce that was in A's request which associates this response with that request; it contains a secret key K_{AB} to be used for communication between A and B; and it contains a 'ticket' (K_{AB}, A, t) encrypted in B's secret key K_B. Encrypted in the ticket is a timestamp t to guarantee freshness.

A sends this 'ticket' and an encrypted nonce to B. B decrypts the 'ticket', obtains the key K_{AB} and then uses this key to send an agreed transformation of A's nonce. B also sends a fresh nonce to A. A is now satisfied that the right B has been reached. The protocol completes with A performing an agreed transformation on B's nonce and sending this transformed nonce to B in a message encrypted with K_{AB}. This seems like quite a lot to do in order to distribute a key securely. However, it is necessary in order to ensure

- that the recipients are the authentic principals, and
- that any messages caught by intruders and replayed would be trapped.

4.5.3 Public key cryptography

Public key encryption is based on the principle of one-way functions. A one-way function $f(x) = y$ has the property that given the value y, it is very difficult to find x. Such a function is used to generate a pair of keys EK and DK. EK, which is used for encryption, is made public; DK, which is used for decryption, is kept private. Since it is very hard to determine DK from EK, DK can be considered secure.

The well-known **RSA** (Rivest, Shamir, Adelman) public key encryption system is based on the difficulty of finding prime factors of very large numbers (numbers greater than 10^{100}). A very useful property of this system is that the keys are commutative, i.e. in addition to being able to encrypt with EK and decrypt with DK, the plaintext can be encrypted with DK and the ciphertext decrypted with EK. The usefulness of this feature will become obvious as you read on.

This deals effectively with the key distribution problem. Any principal A desiring to send a message M to principal B can obtain B's publicly known encode key EK_B. A can then send the encrypted message $EK_B\{M\}$ to B. Since B is the only principal with the private decode key DK_B, no other principal would be able to perform $DK_B\{EK_B\{M\}\}$ and so derive the plaintext M.

However, the issue of authentication remains. How can principal A be sure that principal B is the real B and not an impostor, i.e. does principal A really have principal B's public key? For this reason it is necessary to run a public key authentication protocol.

Public key authentication

Figure 4.11 gives a derivative of the Needham and Schroeder public key authentication protocol. In this protocol a trusted authentication server S handles the public key distribution. The principals know S's public key. Principal A requests B's public key from S to which S responds in a message encrypted in its private key. A then uses S's public key to decrypt the message, retrieve B's public key and send an encrypted message to B. Principal B then obtains A's public key from S. Principals A and B can then check each other out in a pair of encrypted messages.

Public key cryptography is significantly slower than secret key cryptography. Secret key encryption algorithms are known to run 100 to 1000 times faster than public key encryption. Therefore it is good strategy to use public key merely to initiate a communication session and then conduct the session with an agreed secret key.

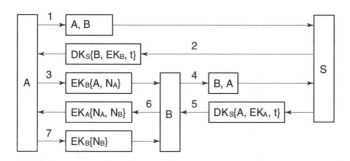

Figure 4.11 Public key authentication protocol derived from Needham–Schroeder.

4.5.4 Digital signatures

Digital signatures are a functional replacement for handwritten signatures. A digital signature allows the principals or a third party to verify, immediately or at some subsequent occasion, that an electronic document was sent from one of the principals to the other. This is an important and necessary feature in electronic commerce and in other electronic communication which can be subject to litigation.

Public key cryptography which employs commutative keys provides a simple mechanism for digital signatures. Principal A can send a signed message M to principal B with two levels of encryption as follows: $EK_B\{DK_A\{M\}\}$, i.e. M is first encrypted with A's private decode key, then this is encrypted with B's public encode key.

On receiving the ciphertext principal B does two levels of decryption, first with B's private decode key, i.e. $DK_B\{EK_B\{DK_A\{M\}\}\}$ to obtain $DK_A\{M\}$, then with A's public encode key, i.e. $EK_A\{DK_A\{M\}\}$ to obtain M. Since A's decode key is known only by A, the ciphertext message $DK_A\{M\}$ could have come only from A. Of course, if A's private key gets into the hands of anyone else the system falls apart, and furthermore, verification can be binding only as long as A maintains the same private key.

Public key digital signatures, as used above, require doubly encrypting the entire message. This could at times be quite an overkill, especially in cases where a digital signature may be necessary, but there is no need for the secrecy provided by encrypting the entire message. In these cases a **message digest** can be used. A message digest function MD transforms the variable-length message M into a fixed-length bit string MD(M) called the message digest, such that

- no two messages will have the same message digest,
- given M it is easy to compute MD(M), and
- given MD(M) it is effectively impossible to generate M.

Principal A can then send a signed message M, $DK_A\{MD(M)\}$ to principal B in a commutative public key system employing message digest. The message M is not encrypted, but the message digest MD(M) is encrypted with A's private decode key. Principal B can then feel confident that the encrypted digest is from A, and since only the original M will produce MD(M) a corrupted or altered M will be trapped. One message digest used heavily on the Internet is **MD5**. MD5 transforms the input message (with appropriate padding) into multiple 512-bit blocks which are used as input to generate a 128-bit message digest.

4.5.5 Kerberos and others

Kerberos is a security system that is based on the Needham–Schroeder secret key protocol. It was developed at MIT initially for their distributed computing

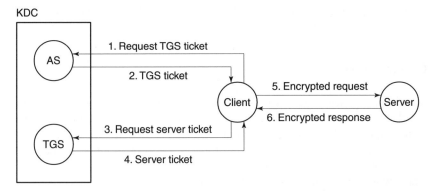

Figure 4.12 In Kerberos the clients must be processed in a Key Distribution Centre (KDC) by an Authentication Server (AS) and a Ticket Granting Server (TGS) to obtain a secret session key for communication with a desired server.

systems and it is now enjoying relatively wide acceptance in other distributed applications. In Kerberos user principals access server principals through client processes. Client–server interaction takes place within a session for which a secret session key must be obtained. The session key is supplied by the Kerberos Key Distribution Centre (KDC).

The KDC is implemented as two servers: an Authentication Server (AS) and a Ticket Granting Server (TGS) (see Figure 4.12). The client is authenticated by the AS and given a ticket containing a secret key for communication with the TGS. The client then communicates with the TGS who supplies a ticket containing a secret key for communication with the desired server. These exchanges follow the Needham–Schroeder protocol closely.

You may have heard of **PGP** and **PEM** in the context of security. These are easily available security systems designed for email. PGP (Pretty Good Privacy), originally developed by Philip Zimmermann, provides privacy, authentication and digital signatures. PGP uses RSA public key encryption and MD5 to generate and transmit the signatures, and IDEA secret key encryption for secure message delivery. PEM (Privacy Enhanced Mail) is an official Internet standard providing facilities similar to PGP. PEM uses RSA and MD5 for authentication and digital signatures, and DES for secure message delivery. Coulouris *et al.* (1994) and Tanenbaum (1996) are good sources for more detail on security in distributed systems and computer networks.

The Secure Sockets Layer (**SSL**) protocol was specified by Netscape (see http://home.netscape.com) as a security protocol for client–server communications over the Internet. SSL is now widely used. The protocol is designed to prevent eavesdropping, tampering and message forgery. SSL runs on top of a reliable transport layer (like TCP) and is application layer independent. SSL uses secret key cryptography (e.g. DES) for data encryption, and public key cryptography (e.g. RSA) for peer authentication. A message digest is computed to ensure message integrity.

4.6 Summary

In distributed systems users access resources that are distributed over computer networks. In the design of a distributed system we must ensure that proper principles and mechanisms are adopted to facilitate the effective management of these distributed resources. This is what this chapter was about. You should now be able to put a good management system in place.

The key issues that must be addressed are

- Naming and addressing
- Sharing
- Availability and reliability
- Replication
- Privacy and security.

Within each of these areas we have highlighted the basic concerns and indicated the methods that can be employed to meet these concerns. Many of these methods are now widely used and in many cases tools are easily obtainable. You are encouraged to use these techniques and tools, and refer to the reading material that is referenced. In the following chapter we shall return to distributed resources, but in that chapter we shall concentrate on the accessing operations or transactions on the resources.

4.7 Questions

1   Identify some key issues that must be addressed in order to manage distributed resources effectively and efficiently.
2   How does a multipart name help in locating a resource in a distributed system?
3   What is a location independent name?
4   What is a capability when used in reference to resource naming?
5   How is partitioning, replication and caching used in the design of a name server?
6   What is the Domain Name System (DNS)?
7   What is an IP address? What is the structure of IP addresses?
8   Distinguish between an Access Control List and a Capability List.
9   What is the distributed shared memory (DSM) model of distributed computing?
10   What concerns relating to the network platform are important when addressing availability and reliability issues in distributed systems?

11 What is the significance of caching in improving the availability of a system?

12 What is the cache coherence problem and how can it be addressed?

13 How can RAID technology improve the performance of a distributed system?

14 How can heavyweight context switching be reduced in concurrent program execution?

15 What are some advantages gained by replicating resources in a distributed system?

16 What key commands must be supported by a group membership service?

17 How is the group *view* used to handle group changes?

18 Name the reliability classes into which multicasting can be divided.

19 Name the classifications that can be used in ordering messages.

20 Give an algorithm that can be used to elect a new leader of a group.

21 Distinguish between centralized sequencing and distributed sequencing of totally ordered multicast.

22 Give a distributed sequencing algorithm that can be used to totally order messages.

23 How can vector timestamps be used to causally order multicasts?

24 What type of ordering divides messages into two mutually exclusive sets at all members of the group?

25 Distinguish between secret key cryptography and public key cryptography.

26 What is the role of the authentication server in key distribution?

27 Explain how a message digest can be used to transmit a digital signature.

28 What is Kerberos? What is the role of the Ticket Granting Server in Kerberos?

29 Refer to the Student Registration system in Question 21 of Chapter 3. Suggest some names that will be recognizable by the system. Recommend a format for these names. How will these names be stored? If the system uses databases, how can these databases be (a) partitioned? (b) replicated? How will access be controlled to ensure privacy and security?

CHAPTER 5

Accessing distributed resources

The resources are now all there, dispersed over the system and ready to be accessed by a wide range of users. These accesses can be expressed as read, execute and write operations, all requiring careful attention to ensure that acceptable results are achieved. The resources, as we have discussed in Chapter 4, must be identifiable, reachable and shareable subject to certain privacy and security controls. Once these are established, accessing can be allowed.

Accessing the resources is from one point of view a communication issue. This we have looked at before but we need to examine it in some more detail. On many occasions there are concurrent accesses to the same resource, which accesses may require some type of synchronization to generate correct final states. Sometimes mutually exclusive access to a resource is required. The issues of global time and coordination are particularly relevant and there is always that question 'What if something fails?'. In this chapter we shall examine these areas under the following headings:

- Communication
- Concurrency
- Time
- Failure.

5.1 Communication

In Chapter 1 (Section 1.3) communication was highlighted as a key issue in distributed system design. Several protocol layers are employed to facilitate the rather ubiquitous user-to-resource interaction that exists at present. In Chapter 3 we saw how distributed systems can be implemented as cooperating processes, process groups or client–server systems using procedure-oriented and object-oriented technologies.

Within these architectures the main forms of communication are remote procedure calling and message passing. These schemes then use the underlying network architecture to get the messages through the communication channels. Section 3.2 examined how TCP/IP and ISO/OSI facilitate this communication.

5.1.1 Remote procedure call (RPC)

In **procedure call**, the calling process issues a call instruction naming the process. Arguments are passed by value or reference to the called process. If both the caller and the called are running in user mode on the same machine, they could be procedures linked together in the same object module. Therefore, the call would involve a jump in execution from one procedure to the other, followed some time after by a return, without the need to enter the kernel of the operating system.

On the other hand, the call may require entry to the kernel, e.g. the called process may be an I/O handler which needs explicit operating system control. The call instruction is, in this case, a system call which causes the entry to the operating system kernel. The kernel transfers the arguments to the address space of the called process. The caller is forced to wait until the called process executes and then replies via the kernel to the calling process.

If the called process resides at a remote site, the arguments must be packaged as a message and transmitted through the network to the destination host, where it is executed as a procedure call, while the caller waits. On completion, the response is relayed back to the caller. This scheme is referred to as **remote procedure call (RPC)**.

Birrell and Nelson (1984) indicated that the RPC mechanism has a number of attractive properties. They claimed that it is based on a well-known technique that is relatively clean and simple; therefore, with RPC, it should be easier to support reliable distributed computation systems. The simplicity should generate an efficiency in design which would provide rapid exchange of information. The present widespread use of RPC is in some way a validation of this claim of Birrell and Nelson.

Five modules interact in the implementation of an RPC system. They are the client (or user), the client-stub (or user-stub), the RPC communications package, the server-stub, and the server (see Figure 5.1).

The client-stub is invoked when the client makes a remote call. This resembles a normal local call. The client-stub assembles one or more packets which will include the target procedure and parameters, and then requests the local instance of the RPC communications package to transmit the packet(s) to the called machine.

The packing of the parameters into a message, which is called **parameter marshalling**, should not be viewed as a trivial task, since semantic integrity has to be preserved across possibly heterogeneous systems. When the remote RPC communications package receives the packets it passes them to the server-stub. The server-stub unpacks and procedure calls the server. During this time, the client who issued the call waits. When the server has finished, the results are relayed via the same path. These five separate program modules allow independent development of the cooperating parts of the RPC system.

RPC is inherently a synchronous protocol: the client calls and blocks, the server is invoked, it processes the call and responds, then the client is unblocked.

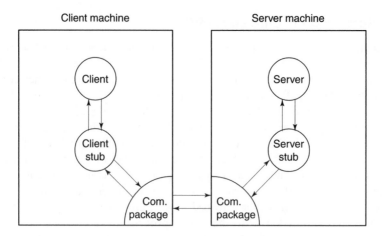

Figure 5.1 RPC with five modules: client, client-stub, server, server-stub and communications package.

However, there are implementations of asynchronous RPC in which multiple requests could be made to a server without the client waiting on a response to each request.

5.1.2 Sun RPC

A widely used RPC system is the Sun RPC. It is used in Sun's Network File System (NFS) and many UNIX implementations. It uses UDP and TCP/IP for packet exchange between client and server.

Remote procedures are owned by servers. These procedures are expressed to the clients in an Interface Definition Language (IDL) as discussed under CORBA in Section 3.1.4. The IDL in Sun RPC is called XDR (eXternal Data Representation).

For example, assume that the RPC system supports remote file reading. Then the server will possess a READFILE procedure that accepts read requests with suitable arguments from clients. This can be expressed as an XDR interface as in Figure 5.2.

This interface stands between the client and the server and is integral to the generation of the client and server stubs shown in Figure 5.1. The interface declares that a client can access procedure no. 1 in version 3 of program no. 777 at a named server to read a file. The file identifier, a pointer to begin reading and the length of the character string to be read must be supplied. The read procedure returns the character string in a Message structure.

The client must first call its local stub procedure. This stub procedure is the local agent of the remote server procedure. The stub procedure carries the same name (but in lower-case and the number appended) as the interface procedure.

```
const MAX=800;
typedef int FileId;
typedef int FilePointer;
typedef int Length;
struct Message {
  int length;
  char buffer[MAX];
};
struct fileargs {
  FileId file;
  FilePointer point;
  Length length;
};

program FILEREAD {
  version VERSION {
    Message READFILE(fileargs) = 1;
  } = 3;
} = 777;
```

Figure 5.2 XDR interface.

Therefore

```
info = readfile_1(&args, clientHandle);
```

can constitute a call to the server via the client stub. The variables `info` and `args` must be declared as `Message` and `fileargs` structures respectively in the calling client program. The item `clientHandle` facilitates binding to the specific service. It allows Sun RPC to use its name service called *port mapper* to resolve the hostname of the server, the program and version numbers on to a port at a remote computer.

The arguments are marshalled and TCP or UDP is used to transmit the request to the server. At the server the corresponding stub listens to the declared port number for incoming requests, which conform to the interface. These requests are unmarshalled and passed on to the identified procedure. Provisions exist for retries in the event of time-outs. Results follow the return path through the stubs.

5.1.3 Message passing

In a **message passing** scheme, all communication is handled as message blocks which the OS kernel undertakes to transfer from a sender process to a receiver process. The kernel may store the message in intermediary buffers before delivering it to the receiver process. The sender process issues a 'send message' command in which it identifies the receiver and the message. The receiver usually must issue an explicit 'receive message' command in which it identifies a sender

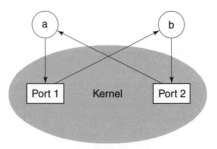

Figure 5.3 Processes **a** and **b** communicate via ports controlled by OS kernel.

and names a data area in its address space for the deposit of the message. Often the messages are sent to and received from established ports which must be used in the addressing (see Figures 5.3 and 5.4).

In order to send a message to another process over the network (as in Figure 5.4), the message goes first to the port of the local 'network server' to be passed to the remote 'network server'. The remote 'network server' then sends it to the port of the receiving process from where it is retrieved when the remote process issues the appropriate 'receive message' command.

Message passing is inherently asynchronous. The issuing of a 'send message' command is not a guarantee of receipt unless there is a specific protocol that provides this guarantee. Issuing of a 'receive message' command may not mean that a message has been sent.

Whether the sender waits on the complete handling of the communication can be determined by the nature of the particular task and not upon the fact that a message passing instruction was issued. No blocking increases the parallelism in execution, but it also increases the programmers' responsibility to ensure correctness. Therefore, some blocking on the sender and receiver processes may be included in the message passing protocol.

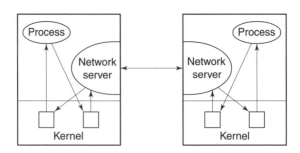

Figure 5.4 Message passing across network using ports.

5.1.4 MPI

The **Message Passing Interface** (**MPI**) is a relatively popular message passing standard with implementations supporting parallel and distributed programming coded mainly in C and Fortran (Dongarra *et al.*, 1996).

Included among the many useful specifications in MPI are the following key standards:

- Point-to-point communications
- Collective communications
- Groups and contexts.

In *point-to-point communication* one process can send a message containing typed data to another process. Types can be chosen from the primitive types like integer or floating-point number, or they may be user-defined types. User-defined types in MPI allow the communicators to describe, through type-constructor functions, the layout in memory of sets of primitive types.

Communicating processes register with a 'communicator' in MPI. The communicator identifies and addresses the processes involved in message exchange. The default communicator in MPI is `MPI_COMM_WORLD`. In the following statement a process sends a message to a process with ID 1:

```
MPI_Send(msg, strlen(msg)+1, MPI_CHAR, 1, tag, MPI_COMM_WORLD)
```

`msg` was declared as a character string, `MPI_CHAR` indicates that the message is of type character, `1` identifies the receiving process, `tag` tags the message to accommodate message selection by the receiver, and the last argument identifies the communicator.

If we assume that the sending process is process 0, then a corresponding receive message from process 0 must be issued by process 1, e.g.,

```
MPI_RECV(msg, 20, MPI_CHAR, 0, tag, MPI_COMM_WORLD, &status)
```

where `20` indicates the maximum length of message expected, and `status` records information on the outcome of the exchange.

Collective communication transmits data among all the processes registered with a communicator. This includes synchronization, broadcast, gather and scatter operations. Synchronization does not exchange data; it synchronizes processes. Broadcast is the 'from one to all' transfer, while gather is a 'from all to one' transfer. In scatter a process separates the data into sets such that each process gets a set.

Groups and *contexts* provide support for process group and group view resembling that discussed in Section 4.4. The processes registered with a 'communicator' define the scope or context of the communication operations, i.e. like a process group. A new context can be created by creating a new 'communicator'. A message sent in one context cannot be received in another context.

MPI allows both blocking and non-blocking message passing. A 'blocking send' blocks the process until the send-message buffer can be reused safely. A 'blocking receive' blocks until the receive-message buffer contains the expected message. Non-blocking behaviour overlaps multiple message transmissions or overlaps a message transmission with computations.

5.1.5 Sockets and streams

In Section 3.2 we discussed network architecture and, in particular, we saw how several layers are used to facilitate the computer-to-computer interactions. We have just seen how RPC and message passing permit the process-to-process interactions. These schemes must employ the communication protocols in the network architecture in order to send and receive information over the network. In fact an interface must be established between the scheme (or process or module) and the network protocol suite.

The protocol suite in relatively common use is TCP/IP (see Section 3.2.8). Therefore, it is often necessary to interface with the transport layer facilities TCP and UDP, that are supported in the TCP/IP architecture. TCP provides a connection-oriented service while UDP provides connectionless datagram service.

Specific issues that the interface must address are:

- How to associate a process or program with a communication channel;
- How to associate a process or program with a connection;
- How to associate a message with a communication channel;
- How to associate a message with a connection;
- What data structure should represent a connection;
- What data structure should represent a message.

A picture that arises is that the interface allows the program to plug into the network. Hence the use of the term **socket**. The socket, pioneered in Berkeley Unix, is now a standard interface to TCP/IP networks and is supported on several platforms (Orfali and Harkey, 1998).

A process that provides a service (i.e. a server) must create a socket through which its service can be reached and delivered. A process requesting a service (i.e. a client) must create a socket to send requests and receive responses. Therefore a socket is inherently bidirectional.

In object-oriented programming a socket is an object with attributes and methods as indicated in Figure 5.5.

The *host-address* is an IP address; the *port-no* associates this socket with a unique process or service at the host; *queue-length* indicates the maximum number of messages that can be pending for processing by this process. In

Attributes
```
Host-address
Port-no
Queue-length
```

Methods
```
Socket Constructor
Bind
Connect
Listen
Accept
Send
Receive
Close
```

Figure 5.5 Socket as object.

particular, a server uses *queue-length* to indicate the maximum number of requests that can be waiting for service.

Socket Constructor creates a socket; *bind* links the process to this socket; *connect* requests that a connection be set up with a remote socket; *listen* indicates readiness to receive incoming messages, e.g. a server listening for incoming requests; *accept* grants a connection to this socket in response to a *connect* request from a remote socket; *send* and *receive* are for message exchange through this socket; and *close* closes the socket.

This socket object will interface with a connection-oriented service. A datagram socket does not require the connection establishment. The messages can also be declared as objects. In the connectionless datagram service the message packets are handled independently of each other and can be declared as in Figure 5.6.

Attributes
```
message-buffer
message-length
address
port-no
```

Methods
```
getAddress
getData
getLength
getPort
setAddress
setData
setLength
setPort
```

Figure 5.6 A datagram object.

In the connection-oriented service message packets must be received at the destination in the same sequence in which they were sent. Therefore the packets can be viewed as being transmitted along a pipe or as a 'stream'. A **stream** object can then be defined for TCP transmissions. The specific stream objects to facilitate sending and receiving over a connection can be inherited from a general stream object facilitating input and output by any process. The Java programming language uses this technique.

Java provides a stream class hierarchy in its `java.io` package. From this package the `OutputStream` class can be used to send data and the `InputStream` class can be used to receive data. Methods `getOutputStream` and `getInput Stream` are provided to obtain references to these streams. The `OutputStream` method `write` and the `InputStream` method `read` can be used to send and receive individual bytes respectively. For example, the Java statements:

```
Socket client;
Inputstream input;
```

declare `client` as socket object and `input` as `InputStream` object; and

```
client = new Socket(address, port-no);
input = client.getInputStream();
chr = input.read();
```

facilitate reading from the socket.

In summary we recall the high-level client–server communication, and the object invocations provided by CORBA, Java-RMI and other tools discussed in Section 3.1, where it was indicated that the primitives used are mainly RPC and message passing. We have now seen how these primitives interact with the network architecture to meet the communication demands.

5.2 Concurrency

Concurrent processing has been a feature of computer systems since the advent of multiprocessing operating systems running on uniprocessor machines. Multiprocessor computers and computer networks now afford vast opportunities for concurrent activity. When concurrent processes share resources conflicts can arise. Information can be corrupted and inconsistent states can be generated. Therefore, it is necessary to control concurrency. Often this means synchronizing interdependent actions and enforcing mutually exclusive access to resources.

In operating system design shared data and procedures form a 'critical section' and several techniques have been proposed and adopted to manage access to critical sections in shared memory systems. There are many good texts on the fundamentals of operating systems which deal effectively with these issues (e.g. Stallings, 1995).

Common approaches include:

- the hardware test-and-set instruction which allows non-interruptible testing and setting of a lock variable;
- Dijkstra's wait and signal on a semaphore which access the semaphore in a disable interrupt sequence;
- Dekker's and Peterson's algorithms which use 'interested' and 'turn' variables to control access to the critical section; and
- monitors which encapsulate the critical section in an identifiable program structure.

Brinch Hansen (1978) proposed the use of *guarded regions* in his *DP* (Distributed Processes) language. DP supported:

(a) a fixed number of concurrent processes that are started simultaneously and exist forever, with each process accessing its own variables;
(b) processes can communicate with each other by calling common procedures defined within processes; and
(c) processes are synchronized by means of *guarded regions*.

A process has the following format:

process name
own variables
common procedures
initial statement

A process begins execution with its initial statement and continues until the statement either terminates or waits for a condition to be satisfied. The common procedures permit external requests from other processes. Therefore, having executed the initial statement the process may start another operation in response to some external request. When this is terminated, or some waiting is necessary, the process may either resume an earlier operation (if some condition waited for has become true) or start a new operation in response to another external request. This can continue forever.

A procedure has the following format:

proc name(input parameters, output parameters)
local variables
statement

A process, A, can call a procedure, C, defined in another process, B, by using a `call` statement, e.g.

```
call B.C(input param, out param)
```

For synchronization of process activity, there is the *guarded region* which involves `when` and `cycle` statements. The `when` statement indicates that the process must wait until a particular condition is true before executing some corresponding statement. The `cycle` statement indicates an endless repetition of a `when` statement.

Brinch Hansen determined how the 'wait' and 'signal' operations on a semaphore initialized to zero can be implemented in DP. Define a process, 'sem', as follows:

```
process sem; s: int
proc wait; when s > 0: s := s-1 end
proc signal; s := s+1
s := 0
```

Other processes can call sem in the following manner:

```
call sem.wait
call sem.signal
```

This is process-level concurrency. We have discussed in Sections 2.5 and 4.3 the efficiency that can be achieved by using thread-level concurrency. When threads share data and procedures the same 'critical section' issue arises, and similar control techniques must be employed. For example, Java uses the monitor structure to enforce thread synchronization.

As indicated above, the monitor is an abstraction of the critical section. For example, if thread A writes to and thread B reads from a common character buffer, then the buffer, the 'write' and 'read' methods would form a monitor to which only one thread at a time has access (see Figure 5.7). In Java a monitor is an object with its methods declared as *synchronized*. To execute a synchronized method a lock must be obtained on the object.

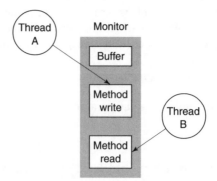

Figure 5.7 Each thread has exclusive access to the monitor to write to/read from the character buffer.

Locking is the customary low-level approach to the implementation of mutually exclusive access to a resource. However, when concurrent processes contend for the use of the same resources a **deadlock** can occur. This can be aggravated in the distributed system where there can be contention for resources scattered over the network.

5.2.1 Distributed deadlock

A deadlock exists when some process A holds on to a resource X while waiting on some resource Y, which will not be released by a process B until process A releases X (see Figure 5.8). The deadlock situation in which the processes and resources involved are dispersed over the network is called *distributed deadlock*. As in the centralized system, one may choose to ignore, prevent, avoid or detect deadlocks. Prevention and detection are possibly the more commonly used strategies.

The detection strategy accepts the possibility of deadlock occurrence and employs some mechanism to track down and then break the deadlock. The basic detection procedure is to look for a cycle in a resource allocation graph (see Figure 5.9). Following the path from process to resource to process can take one across several nodes. The search for a cycle can be initiated whenever a process blocks on a resource. If a cycle is discovered a selection scheme must be employed to determine which process should be pre-empted (i.e. should give up resources). One selection procedure is to collect the IDs or numbers of all the processes in the cycle, and pre-empt the process with the highest number.

Prevention aims to allocate resources in such a manner that a deadlock will never occur. Among the techniques that can be employed to effect this is to globally order all the resources, and then allocate the resources in increasing order. That is, a process cannot hold a higher numbered resource while waiting for a lower one. Although this achieves prevention of deadlock, it imposes a serious constraint on the use of resources.

Alternative approaches include the global ordering of the processes by using globally unique *timestamps*, or by employing the **two-phase lock** algorithm.

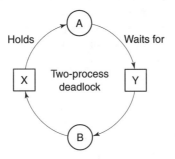

Figure 5.8 Process A holds X and waits for Y; B holds Y and waits for X.

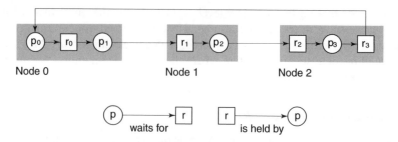

Figure 5.9 Distributed deadlock.

5.2.2 Timestamps

In this context timestamping is a mechanism for enforcing ordered access to shared resources. This implies that a priority in the allocation of a resource must be established. For example, the lower-numbered (or older) process could be given higher priority than the higher-numbered (or younger) process.

Although we use the word 'timestamp', any numbering system that affords the desired ordering would suffice. This we have dealt with already in some detail under 'Message ordering' in Section 4.4. However, a physical clock can be employed in some situations. This we will look at in Section 5.3 under 'Time'.

5.2.3 Two-phase lock

In two-phase lock (2PL) a process must acquire locks on all the required resources in the first phase. In the second phase the locks are released. Having released a lock, a process cannot obtain a lock on the same or any other resource. Since lock acquisition and lock release are mutually exclusive, a process cannot begin execution before locking all requested resources.

But how can this be implemented in the face of other processes trying simultaneously to lock some or all of these very resources which are dispersed around the network? An effective approach is the use of a **centralized lock controller**. A centralized lock controller is a central node which is allowed the function of granting lock requests. A process must first indicate the need to lock the required resources to the central lock controller. If none of these resources is already locked, the lock request is granted; otherwise the new arrival must wait.

5.2.4 Replica control

The resources accessed by concurrent processes in a distributed system are often replicated. For example, it is often necessary to perform update operations to replicas in a distributed database system. We have dealt in some detail with replication in distributed systems in Section 4.4. In this section we address merely the control of concurrent processing.

The two-phase lock and timestamping schemes can also work where there are replicas. All copies of the object involved in the processing can be included in the lock agreement. This means that, in spite of there being multiple copies, no access is allowed to any, until all copies are locked. This can be unnecessarily restrictive, therefore other approaches are often preferred.

Majority consensus

The use of timestamps can be incorporated into another scheme called **majority consensus** (Thomas, 1979). When an update (a write) is applied, its timestamp is recorded. Timestamped operations are broadcast to all hosts holding replicas. If timestamps do not match with previous entries, the updates are accepted to be applied only if there is acceptance by the majority. In this way, the operation held by a minority of the hosts is forced to *back-off*, thus giving way to the majority holder.

Voting

Gifford (1979) proposed a voting scheme where each copy i of the replicated object has a number v_i of votes and v_i can vary across copies. To read that object a transaction must obtain a read quorum of r votes; and to write, a write quorum of w votes such that

$$r + w > \sum v_i, \quad i = 1 \ldots n$$

and

$$w > n/2$$

where n is the number of copies of the object.

The values r, w and v_i can be adjusted either to improve availability or to increase the rate at which consistency is achieved. The write quorum ensures that there is always a subset of copies that are up-to-date. Since the read quorum must intersect the write quorum there is always an up-to-date copy to be read. Version numbers are used for ageing the copies. Voting has proved to be an attractive approach in dealing with failures in the network (see Section 5.4).

Primary node

A further approach is the notion of a **primary node** or **primary site**. In this scheme, a single node is identified as the first site where the update is performed (Ullman, 1982).

This concept builds on the geographically clustered behaviour of updates. For example, in a network of bank branches, each branch will deal with many more transactions pertaining to its local accounts than with transactions for a remote branch. Hence, each branch can be allocated as the primary site for all updates to their accounts. The update is then broadcast to the other nodes which perform the update and then send acknowledgements back to the primary node.

Optimistic schemes

The schemes that we have looked at thus far can be classified as **pessimistic protocols**. This classification is appropriate since these schemes assume something can go wrong, and so a strategy is employed, before processing, to prevent the corruption of the data. An **optimistic scheme** assumes that there is little or no chance of something going wrong. Therefore, the operation can be performed before multi-site agreement, with subsequent checking for correctness or consistency. In the event that an undesirable effect is produced, some mechanism for recovery should be employed.

Three effective optimistic approaches are *typing of transactions* (Farrag and Ozsu, 1989; Liskov and Ladin, 1986), *version vectors* (Davidson *et al.*, 1985) and *cost bounds* (Lynch *et al.*, 1986; Crichlow, 1994; Francis and Crichlow, 1995). The 'typing of transactions' approach determines from semantic knowledge of the transaction whether it is safe to execute it without agreement (see Section 6.2 for more on transactions).

Version vectors (or version timestamps as discussed under 'causally ordered multicast' in Section 4.4) allow the updates on a replica to be counted in order to determine conflicts. Each replica maintains a vector of n entries, where n is the number of replicas. The entry in position i indicates the number of updates to the replica originating from site i. If all the entries of the version vector of one site i are greater than or equal to the corresponding entries of the version vector of the other site j, then i can adjust j's version. If this relationship is not satisfied then the two vectors are said to conflict and the inconsistency has to be resolved.

The 'cost bounds' approach associates a cost value (bound) with the data fields that can be altered by a write. A write can then be allowed to proceed as long as the change it would generate to that data field is less than or equal to the cost bound.

5.3 Time

Time provides an effective means for scheduling, recording and ordering events. To meet these requirements, a frame of reference or context must be established, a begin indicator must be defined and an incremental point for counting time (possibly forever) must be agreed upon. For example, the rhythmic beating of a drum may work well for coordinating a musical event. However, the drum-beat would not work to coordinate simultaneously two musical events located outside the audio range of each other.

Therefore, a distinction can be made between time within some single domain and time across many domains. The distinction is manifest in the procedures involved in establishing synchronization. In our everyday lives we often use globally synchronized clocks to meet our timing needs. However, we know that at times keeping the clocks synchronized could be quite a pain. Happily, correctly synchronized physical clocks are not always necessary.

5.3.1 Logical clocks

In distributed systems it is often necessary to order message passing. We discussed this in Section 4.4 where we examined causally ordered and totally ordered multicast. The totally ordered multicast used a numbering protocol (without the help of a physical clock) to order the message passing in a group of processes. This protocol is based on Lamport's (1990) *logical clock* algorithm.

The notion of the logical clock arises since the objective is not to tell what time of the day it is but rather to establish a 'happened before' relationship, for which a physical clock is not necessary. The underlying principles are as follows:

1   Within any sequential process it can be observed that an event a happened before an event b.
2   If event a is the sending of a message from one process and event b is the receiving of that message by another process, then a happened before b.

Upon these principles one can assign logical time $C(a)$ to any event a, such that if a happened before b, then $C(a) < C(b)$. To effect this, Lamport proposed that each process in the distributed system should maintain a simple counter (a logical clock) which must be incremented (by at least 1) on every event. Since time does not go backward the counter cannot be decremented.

Logical clocks can run at different rates at separate sites. It is therefore possible that a message sent from some process A to another process B can arrive at a time earlier than it was sent if the logical clock at A is ticking faster than the logical clock at B. To correct this, any message a must be timestamped with the current time $C(a)$ of the sending process. On receiving the message its timestamp $C(a)$ is compared with the current time t of the receiver process. Since the send event 'happened before' the receive event, then t must be greater than $C(a)$. If this is not the case t must be corrected to read at least $C(a) + 1$.

In order to support total ordering no two events can have the same time. To achieve this the logical clock should not only tick at least once between events but also record the time as a concatenated timestamp generated by attaching to the count a decimal point followed by the process number. For example, the logical clock at process 1 should show time like 0.1, 1.1, 2.1, …; the logical clock at process 2 should show time like 0.2, 1.2, 2.2, and so on.

5.3.2 *Physical clocks*

In the distributed system a key issue regarding time is that all the nodes involved must be able to agree on 'the time at which an event occurred'. This can be resolved by using physical clocks if either

(a)   all the clocks show the correct time at all times, or
(b)   clocks show different time but there exists a trusted time-keeper that always knows the correct time.

With physical clocks the correct time is a time-of-day indicator to an agreed degree of accuracy (possibly seconds, milliseconds, etc.). The global correct time is known as **Universal Coordinated Time** (abbreviated **UTC**) and this can be obtained via specific shortwave radio or satellite services.

That all clocks would show the correct time at all times is an unrealistic assumption. Clocks count time at different rates, i.e. they are subject to *clock drift*. Hence it is necessary to synchronize the clocks repeatedly. If there are many nodes involved in the distributed system, then synchronization which involves each clock listening periodically to a UTC service is an expensive (and probably unjustifiable) option.

Therefore, at least one node – the time-keeper or *time server* – should listen to a UTC service and the other nodes would synchronize their clocks with the time server. Several clock synchronization algorithms are available. Two representative algorithms are Cristian and Berkeley (Coulouris *et al.*, 1994). Fundamental to each algorithm is the exchange of messages between the time server and the other nodes, and hence the need to have a good estimate of the round-trip time delay for message exchange between server and each node.

In *Cristian's algorithm* a node periodically obtains the time t_{server} from the time server. The node will then compute what should be the correct time t, where

$$t = t_{\text{server}} + \Delta t$$

and Δt is a compensation based on the message transmission time. If *min*, the minimum one-way message transmission delay between node and server, is known, and the measured round-trip delay is *round* then Δt is in the range [*min*, *round* − *min*]. Several requests can be made from which the minimum value of *round* can be selected.

In the *Berkeley algorithm* the time server polls the other nodes periodically to obtain their clock readings. When these readings are obtained, an estimate of round-trip delay to each node is considered in order to determine the current times shown by each of the polled nodes. The time server then uses these times and its own clock's time to compute an average time-of-day. This average *ave.t* is then viewed by the time server as the correct time.

All the clocks in the system must now be synchronized by using *ave.t*. However, instead of sending *ave.t* to the other nodes, the time server estimates a difference dt_i (positive or negative) by which each node i must correct its time, and sends this difference to the appropriate nodes. Since a faulty clock (which has drifted badly or shows a spurious reading) can have an adverse effect on the computation of the average, the algorithm averages over a subset of readings that differ from each other only by a specified amount.

Clock synchronization can be performed over the Internet by using the **Network Time Protocol (NTP)**. Time servers in NTP form a logical hierarchy of top-level primary servers and lower-level secondary servers. Servers at one level are synchronized from servers at the level above; primary servers listen directly to a UTC service. Statistical techniques are used to compensate for clock drift and message transmission times. Redundant servers exist to afford increased reliability, and authentication schemes are employed to establish trusted time servers.

5.4 Failure

There are several issues of failure which arise within the context of 'accessing distributed resources'. Messages can be lost. These messages may be conveying requests from clients, responses from servers, or interactions among members of a process group. A node may fail during an access operation. That node may be a client, it may be a server, or it may be the member of a process group. The failure can partition the network such that some operable nodes can no longer reach other operable nodes.

5.4.1 Lost messages

A message is considered lost by the sender if an outcome associated with the receipt of that message has not materialized. Since the sender would not be waiting indefinitely for the outcome then messages which are inordinately delayed (due to network traffic conditions) will fall into this category. So too will some messages that get corrupted during transmission and hence are rejected, and the messages that are dumped due to full queues at the destination or at intermediary nodes.

The loss of messages is normally dealt with by setting time-out intervals and resending the message some number of times. Since, unknown to the sender, the original may have been received, the receiver must be able to distinguish the original message from a retransmission. We addressed a similar issue in frame management under the 'data link layer' in Section 3.2.2.

Sequentially numbering (or timestamping) the messages is a useful technique that can be employed to distinguish messages. A retransmitted message will carry the same number as the original. Therefore, on receiving a message, its timestamp can be compared with those already received to determine if it is a repeat, in which event it will be rejected.

This rather simple sounding procedure is not without some problems. What is the allowable range of numbers? Since the system may have been designed to live 'forever' then the timestamp field should be pretty big. For how long can a message get stuck somewhere in the network and then turn up at your 'doorstep'? This 'lost' time will determine how many timestamps of received messages will have to be saved in order to be able to spot the duplicate messages. Furthermore, what if a node crashes and loses its record of numbers?

These issues have been addressed in different ways. As we have discussed above, logical or physical clocks could be used to number a message on initiation. A fixed-size field for the timestamp has to be chosen with a life-span in mind. The network should be able to spot old messages and kill them off.

With respect to keeping a history of timestamps, this can be avoided if processing is done in some order, in which case a node then knows which message to expect next. If an arriving message does not carry the expected number, that message will be discarded. On the other hand, the receiving node can keep a record of the last number received and discard any arriving message with a timestamp that is less than or equal to the last one recorded.

Client–server interaction

The lost message can be a lost request from a client or a lost response from a server. These cases have been dealt with already in Section 3.1.3. It is necessary to ensure that the server is not fooled into repeating operations which when repeated compromise the integrity of the system. The *three-message* and *single-shot* protocols were highlighted as appropriate procedures to be employed in this area.

5.4.2 Failed nodes

A node may fail while participating in a 'resource access' operation. We are considering crash failure, i.e. the node stops operating with a clean break between being operational and not operational. The node may have sent a request, then crashed, or it may have received a request for service and crashed before fulfilling the request. The node may be a member of a group cooperating on an operation, e.g. the update of a number of replicas.

A failed node cannot declare that it has failed. Therefore, in the distributed system, the issue of identifying failed nodes has to be addressed. This is even more critical if the failed node is a coordinator or leader. This is resolved within the context of message exchanges. We have examined this already under 'Reliability of message delivery' in Section 4.4.2.

If a node fails while processing, information can be lost. If a record of timestamps of received messages is being kept, this and other state information can be lost. Data areas can get corrupted as a result of incomplete writes. One way to avoid the loss of state information is to keep no state information in the first place, that is, to let the node be a **stateless** node. In this mode all of the node's operations are repeatable.

However, in many cases there is a need to record state and other data and to establish back-ups and other support mechanisms to facilitate recovery from failure. Non-volatile storage is often used as an effective means of back-up; or a recovering node may be refreshed from a live node. View changes, as discussed in Section 4.4, can be used to bring nodes back into synchronization. Furthermore, the principle of *atomic update* can be employed to handle failure during writes.

An atomic update has the guarantee that either the update succeeded and a new state is generated or the update failed and the initial (or old) state has been preserved. This falls within the area of atomic transactions which we shall discuss under 'Transactions' in Chapter 6, Section 6.2. There we shall also discuss the **two-phase commit** protocol. The two-phase commit protocol allows several nodes to participate in performing an atomic transaction.

In Section 5.2 we looked at the concurrent processing of accesses and indicated that some schemes required that all the replicas be available before processing was allowed. Such schemes would fail to deliver when a node that contains a replica fails. In order to process beyond node failure the protocol must adjust to the number of copies available. In fact a protocol which allows read access to any copy and write access to all available copies is called an **available copies (AC) protocol** (Bernstein *et al.*, 1987; Paris and Long, 1990).

Since in an AC protocol all writes are multicast to all live replicas, processing can continue as long as one live replica remains accessible. However, the assumption is that a replica that is inaccessible has failed. This may not always be the case, since a node could be inaccessible due to communication failure. Therefore, the protocol does not guarantee data consistency in the presence of communication failures. This could be quite a headache if the system is on a point-to-point network. However, if the network has physical broadcast capability, communication failure often means the whole network is down, which means that no replica can be reached.

5.4.3 Partitioning

In a computer network supporting a distributed system a node or communication link failure can segment the system such that global communication in the distributed system is no longer possible. The sites in the system can then be viewed as existing in separate non-communicating partitions (see Figure 5.10).

Alternative mechanisms exist for processing the accesses to resources in such a partitioned system. This is of special concern if the partitioning separates replicas, e.g. the copies of a database in a distributed database system. For data consistency it is not uncommon to restrict processing to a single partition. This partition is sometimes called the 'distinguished partition'. Of major concern are:

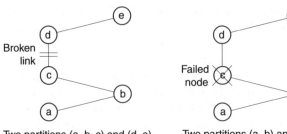

Figure 5.10 Network partitioning.

(a) how to handle accesses that originate in the non-distinguished partition(s), and

(b) how to restore the non-distinguished partition(s), when the failure has been repaired, to a state consistent with the rest of the system.

Quorum or *vote adjustment* schemes allow operable nodes to change their vote (see '*Voting*' in Section 5.2) or quorum assignments when they can no longer communicate with the entire network. Such reassignment may be consensus driven, i.e. communicating nodes determine the new operable topology and together determine a new voting scheme. On the other hand, nodes may be permitted autonomous reassignment of votes.

Each node decides independently when it is time to reassign and does so in accordance with some policy. For example, if a node i cannot communicate with node j then the policy might be to allow node i to add node j's votes to its own. This autonomous approach may not produce as good an assignment as group consensus, but it is faster, simpler, more flexible and it is not impossible to find sensible reassignment algorithms.

Jajodia and Mutchler (1990) proposed *dynamic voting* algorithms which, they contend, provide improved availability over other voting schemes. Their algorithms are called *dynamic voting* and *dynamic–linear*. In dynamic voting there is a version number associated with each copy of the replicated data area or file. The version number is initially zero and is incremented by 1 at each update to the copy. In addition, an integer variable called the 'update sites cardinality' is also associated with each copy of the file. This variable is equal to the number of sites that participated in the most recent update to the file.

Therefore, if 12 is the highest version number in a partition and the update sites cardinality corresponding to the copy with that version number is 5, there must be at least three sites in that partition with version number 12 to allow a further update. It follows, therefore, that updates can proceed in cases where a partition does not contain a majority of the sites holding copies of a file.

Dynamic–linear adds a third variable, 'distinguished site', to each site holding a copy of the file. All the sites participating in an update must agree on a site as the distinguished site. For example, if the sites are linearly ordered the participating site that is greatest in the order can be chosen as the distinguished site. In the event that an even number of sites participated in an update, and a subsequent partition contained half of those sites, dynamic linear allows updates to proceed in the partition with the distinguished site. This increases availability over that permitted in the pure dynamic voting scheme.

Optimistic schemes, as discussed above, allow processing to continue in more than one partition. Whether processing is done in one partition or more than one partition, global inconsistencies are generated. When the failure has been repaired some recovery process must be undertaken.

The fundamental steps here are to identify the inconsistencies that developed during the failure phase, and to initiate a series of updates to bring the system to an acceptable state. During these updates, some replicas should be locked to avoid unpredictable modifications to the data fields. The identification of the updates is facilitated by proper timekeeping logs, indicating when changes were made and when the failure occurred, held at the participating hosts.

5.5 Summary

A distributed system facilitates local and remote access to resources. These accesses traverse a communication network that can at times be very reliable but on other occasions be rather unfriendly. The distributed system designer must ensure that the users of the system are relatively happy with the quality of service delivered, in spite of the behaviour of the subsystems.

In order to achieve this goal it is necessary to address pertinent functional issues. We have highlighted four of these key issues in this chapter. They are communication, concurrency, time and failure. We have shown how they relate to the areas discussed before, particularly under the theme 'Managing distributed resources'.

Under communication we looked at Remote Procedure Calling and Message Passing as basic communication schemes and showed how these have been implemented in some commonly used procedure-oriented and object-oriented tools. Concurrency control is necessary in order to ensure that consistent states are maintained across data resources.

Often the objective is to order the accesses to resources in order to achieve synchronized behaviour or mutually exclusive access to a resource. The notion of time is important in establishing order and synchronized activity. Keeping the right time among widely dispersed nodes requires special algorithms. These algorithms may employ logical clocks or physical clocks.

Messages can get lost, nodes can fail, communication links can go down, and all can occur at unexpected moments. If the system is for the real world then it must survive some failure. We have indicated measures that can be adopted to deal with lost messages and crash-type failures which can occur while accessing resources in a distributed system.

5.6 Questions

1   What are the main forms of communication used by software modules in a distributed system?
2   What is the function of the client-stub in Remote Procedure Call?
3   What is the function of a port in a message passing system?
4   What is the relationship between a 'socket' and a TCP/IP connection?
5   What is the relationship between a 'stream object' and a TCP/IP connection?
6   What is a 'critical section' in concurrent processes?
7   How can a 'monitor' be used to enforce thread-level synchronization?
8   What is distributed deadlock?
9   Explain a detection strategy for controlling distributed deadlock.
10 How can (a) timestamps and (b) two-phase lock be used in distributed concurrency control?
11 Explain the following schemes that can be used for replica control: majority consensus, voting, primary node.
12 Indicate some optimistic schemes that can be used in distributed concurrency control.
13 Distinguish between logical clocks and physical clocks.
14 A message x is sent from process A at logical time $C(x)$ to a remote process B, at which the message arrives at time t. If t is less than $C(x)$ what should process B do to its logical clock?
15 How is a 'time server' used in (a) Cristian's algorithm, and (b) Berkeley's algorithm?
16 What are the conditions that can cause the sender of a message to classify that message as lost?
17 What problem could arise from the retransmission of messages that are assumed lost?
18 What is an atomic update?
19 How can two-phase commit help in ensuring atomic updates?
20 What is an 'available copies' protocol?
21 What is the 'distinguished partition' in a partitioned network?
22 Show how a voting scheme can be used to facilitate processing when the network is partitioned.
23 Refer to the Student Registration system in Question 29 of Chapter 4. What language or software tools would you employ to code the system? Why? How would the program modules interact with each other? How will concurrency be managed? Are there any important timing considerations? How many computers must fail before the Student Registration system cannot deliver any service?

CHAPTER 6

Special issues in resource use

Distributed systems facilitate access to resources irrespective of where these resources may reside on the computer network platform. This should be a painless and fruitful exercise for the authentic users of the system, but a frustrating one for the ill-intentioned. In Chapters 4 and 5 we looked in some detail at how these resources can be managed to produce the kind of behaviour that is acceptable to those who have rights of access, and to create an effective security shield against those without such rights.

Many of the issues touched on in those two chapters lend themselves to more in-depth treatment. Among them there are two areas that are of particular significance, primarily because of their adoption in many distributed systems. These are **distributed shared memory** and **transactions**. Distributed shared memory can be treated as a resource management issue, while transactions can be seen as a resource accessing issue.

6.1 Distributed shared memory

In Section 3.1 we discussed the concept of an executing process. Many computer programs are executed as concurrent processes. These processes may share variables and procedures. For example, one process may write to a character-buffer from which a second process may read. In object-oriented programming this behaviour can be expressed as shared access to a character-buffer object via the invocation of its 'write' and 'read' methods.

On a uniprocessor computer with a single memory module and in shared memory multiprocessors the shared buffer and procedures may be stored in one location and the shared accesses are controlled to ensure correct processing. This is called 'critical section' management in operating systems and there is a considerable body of literature surrounding it (see Section 5.2 on 'Concurrency').

In terms of implementation, a shared memory multiprocessor differs from the uniprocessor. In the shared memory multiprocessor the processors and separate memory modules are connected via a fast interconnection network. However, the hardware is designed such that all processors have right of access to all of

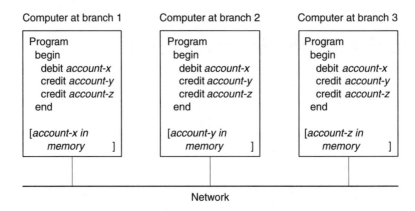

Figure 6.1 DSM lets concurrent programs, running on separate computers, access distributed memory as if it were a single shared memory.

memory. Therefore the singly stored shared buffer is reachable (not necessarily uniformly) from all the processors (see Crichlow, 1997).

This situation is different in the computer network. Here each computer has its own primary memory and any interaction among the computers must involve the communication network protocols. The memory in this arrangement is classified as distributed. However, mechanisms can be employed to present to the programmer an executing environment that behaves like a single shared memory. This is a distributed shared memory (**DSM**) system.

DSM is considered to be useful to the programmer, who can then use the network as if it is a single computer. For example, given a bank with a number of branches where a transaction processing system is to be designed to facilitate transactions on all accounts from 'anywhere', DSM would allow the concurrent (transaction handling) programs running at separate nodes to manipulate account records in a uniform way irrespective of where they are stored (see Figure 6.1).

Another example is that of a distributed real-time system where several processes running at different nodes can be monitoring separate devices and writing to common memory buffers. These buffers can be distributed over several memory modules (see Sections 1.2 and 2.3). These examples can be abstracted onto the 'critical section' problem indicated above.

Shareable unit

DSM must provide a way to globally identify each shareable unit of memory. DSM must maintain a registry (or library) of the shareable units so as to facilitate transparent mapping of program references onto the shared units. All of the communication protocols (like RPC and Message Passing) and the network protocols (like TCP/IP, ISO/OSI, etc.) must be hidden from the programmer.

The unit that is shared in DSM can be a physical block of memory or a logical data structure. The physical block shared in DSM is related to paged virtual memory systems. Data structures shared include variables, procedures and objects. Irrespective of the unit that is shared in DSM, it is necessary to adopt procedures to

(a) synchronize the accesses to shared memory, and
(b) preserve an acceptable level of consistency.

Synchronization

The synchronization procedures that are employed in DSM are chosen from those discussed in Section 5.2, 'Concurrency'. These include the well-tested methods such as monitors, guarded regions, several versions of locks, etc. Some systems hide the synchronization procedures from the programmers, while others provide high-level operations which the programmers use to enforce the desired synchronized behaviour.

Consistency

Consistency procedures are chosen from those discussed in Section 4.4 on 'Replication' and in Section 4.3 on 'Availability and reliability' (under cache coherence). DSM recognizes that applications may be satisfied with different levels of agreement among replicated data. This is captured as different consistency conditions which can be associated with specific consistency models. Primary consistency models used in DSM are *sequential consistency* and *release consistency*.

Sequential consistency

Applications running on DSM can be programmed as cooperating processes. These processes (possibly running on separate computers) may be programmed to issue reads and writes in an order that the programmer considers correct. Sequential consistency ensures that the memory operations associated with these reads and writes occur in the order expected by the programmer.

For example, given that a process contains the code sequence in Figure 6.2, then the expectation of the programmer is that the condition $a \geqslant b$ will always

```
Process
  begin
    a = 0
    b = 0
    a = a + 1
    b = b + 1
  end
```

Figure 6.2 Process sequence to ensure that $a \geqslant b$ will always hold.

hold. This can be guaranteed if the process is running on a uniprocessor computer with its own dedicated primary memory.

However, if a and b are in a shared memory, possibly located at a remote node or even replicated, then the message(s) to perform the updates transmitted over the network can be delivered out of order. Therefore, it is possible that the condition $a \geqslant b$ will not always be satisfied.

A sequentially consistent DSM provides the guarantee that in an example like this the condition $a \geqslant b$ will always hold. This assumption can be made by any other process participating in an application where this is the expectation.

Release consistency

Sequential consistency is a strong consistency model and is relatively costly to implement. Individual updates must be multicast among nodes holding replicas or cached copies. Where applicable the weaker and less costly release consistency model can be implemented.

In release consistency some of the responsibility for maintaining consistency rests with the programmers who are using the DSM system. Synchronization operations (e.g. 'acquire-lock()', 'release-lock()') are made available for processes to use when accessing shareable entities. These synchronization operations establish critical sections (as defined in Section 5.2 and above). The DSM system then uses these synchronization operations to provide sequential consistency at the level of critical sections only.

Programmers are required to know what must be synchronized and to identify this by employing the synchronization operations. If a process accesses a shared variable without the use of synchronization operations then no consistency is guaranteed.

Given the process sequence in Figure 6.3, if the lock acquisition request is successful, then mutually exclusive access is granted to this process to update a and b. The issuing of the 'release-lock' operation will cause the DSM system to economically propagate the updates to any replicas before removing the lock.

Note that the updates are propagated only on the issuing of 'release-lock'. This is release consistency. Since the individual updates need not be

```
Process
  begin
    acquire-lock(CS)
    a = a + 1
    b = b + 1
    release-lock(CS)
  end
```

Figure 6.3 Process requests mutually exclusive access to shared memory.
CS is critical section.

transmitted in separate messages, there are savings on communication and other overhead.

6.1.1 Page-based DSM

Paged DSM has properties similar to paged Virtual Memory (VM) systems on single computers (Li and Hudak, 1989). In a paged VM system there are the virtual memory (secondary storage) and the real memory (primary storage). All the memory (virtual and real) is divided into equally sized blocks called pages. The address space of a process (executable code and data areas) is expressed as some number of these pages, and all address references made by the process have two parameters: (page number, byte number within page).

Processes in execution may occupy virtual memory and their address references are therefore virtual. For the process to run, some subset of its pages must be loaded into real memory initially and subsequent pages may be loaded on demand to complete the execution of instructions fetched from previously loaded pages. In order to facilitate this, the virtual memory pages must be mapped onto the real memory and address translation must be done dynamically. The mapping is supported by Page Map Tables (PMT), and the address translation is done by a special hardware Memory Management Unit (MMU) (see Figure 6.4).

Paged DSM uses software to extend the virtual memory concept to include the memories at remote computers. Shared memory at all of the participating nodes is divided into fixed-size pages. The address space of a process can include both local and remote pages. When a running process references an address that is not in a loaded page, a page fault interrupt occurs and DSM is invoked. If the reference is to a remote page, DSM fetches the page and loads it into the local memory of the requesting process.

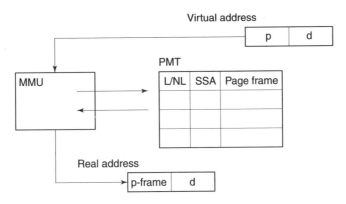

Figure 6.4 Virtual address (p: page number, d: byte displacement) is translated into a real address. The Memory Management Unit (MMU) uses the Page Map Table (PMT) of the running process. The PMT entries indicated are Loaded/Not-loaded (L/NL), Secondary Storage Address of page (SSA) and page frame number in real memory.

Page manager

A basic paged DSM architecture includes a *Page Manager* that maintains a page table of entries for all shared pages in the global memory. The PMT entries for shared pages to be accessed by any process will then point to the appropriate entries in the Page Manager's page table (see Figure 6.5). The Page Manager can be replicated, but for simplicity in design a single Page Manager may exist at a specified node.

The size of a page must be carefully chosen. Longer pages would require longer messages to transmit these pages across the network. Shorter pages can generate more page faults due to the higher frequency of references to unloaded data. Shorter pages also mean more page table entries and more message transmissions.

False sharing

A significant disadvantage in paged DSM is the issue of *false sharing*. Paged DSM shares physical blocks. Processes share logical entities such as variables, data structures, procedures, etc. Paging is transparent, i.e. it just slices up the address space into fixed-size pieces. Therefore, even though a process requires access to only 32 bytes of data, it will get the whole page (probably 512 bytes).

False sharing arises when another process requires access to a separate unrelated data area (probably also 32 bytes long) in this very page (see Figure 6.6). Even though the two processes are not sharing any data, they are forced to share the page. Indeed more than two processes can be accessing unrelated portions of the same page. This has implications for movement and update of pages. The larger the page size the more acute is this problem.

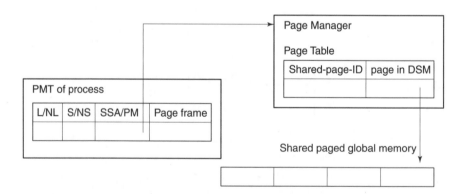

Figure 6.5 Process PMT entries indicate loaded/not-loaded (L/NL),
shared/not-shared (S/NS), if not-shared the secondary storage address (SSA),
if shared the link to the DSM Page Manager (PM), and if loaded the page frame
number in the local memory.

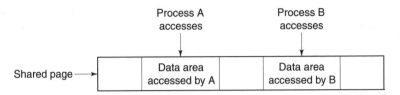

Figure 6.6 In false sharing processes share a page in order to access unrelated data areas.

6.1.2 Logical DSM

There are advantages in sharing a logical data structure rather than a physical block of memory. The problem of false sharing, if not eliminated, can be reduced significantly, and there is potential for increased performance in handling replication and updates. Processes accessing distributed memory can share variables, procedures, records and other structures. There are many DSM projects providing logical sharing. Two interesting examples are the sharing of set-like structures in Linda and the sharing of objects in Orca.

Linda

Linda provides a set of simple operations that embody the 'tuple-space' model of parallel programming. These operations are designed to be incorporated into a base language, thus allowing the writing of parallel programs with the tuple-space model (see Carriero and Galernter, 1989).

The tuple-space (TS) is Linda's model of shared memory. It consists of two types of logical tuples: process tuples and data tuples. Process tuples are active and can execute; data tuples are passive. Process tuples can execute simultaneously and interact by generating, reading and consuming data tuples. When a process tuple is finished executing it turns into a data tuple.

There are four basic primitives in Linda:

(a) *out*(t) – add the tuple t to TS;
(b) *in*(t) – remove a matching tuple from the tuple space. If there is no matching tuple, suspend until one does match;
(c) *rd*(t) – like *in*, but do not remove the tuple; and
(d) *eval*(t) – the same as *out*, except that t is evaluated after rather than before it enters TS.

A tuple is a series of typed fields, e.g.

```
(24, 2.7, "a string")
```

is a tuple of an integer, a real number and a character string. The fields may be actual values or formal parameters, e.g.

```
(200, i: integer, c: character)
```

The operation

```
out(200, i: integer, c: character)
```

causes this tuple to be generated and added to TS. A procedure can select this tuple as an argument list by issuing an `in` operation, e.g.

```
in(200, i: integer, c: character)
```

A tuple created using `eval` resolves into a data tuple, but not before performing any computation specified by its fields. For example,

```
eval("c", 12 * 5, exp(3))
```

creates a three-element 'live tuple' which computes the value of the string "c", multiplies 12 by 5, and raises e to the third power.

Linda has been embedded in a number of languages including Fortran and C; efficient Linda implementations are available on commercial parallel machines; and several applications ranging from the numerical to expert systems have used Linda.

Orca

Orca is an object-based, language-based DSM. Programmers use the Orca language to access Orca managed objects (see Section 3.1.4 for an explanation of objects). Orca is a relatively mature DSM, implemented on a variety of multicomputers and workstation clusters. Bal *et al.* (1998) discuss the performance of Orca and highlight the features of other key DSM systems.

Its portability is obtained through its layered design. The lower layers form a virtual machine called Panda upon which is implemented the Orca runtime system. Orca as a language allows the runtime to benefit from compiler support. For example, at compile time the access patterns to shared objects can be generated and used in making decisions concerning the replication of shared objects.

The shared objects can be accessed only through the user-defined operations on those objects. For example,

```
S$pop(6);
```

invokes the operation *pop* on the stack-defined object *S*. Orca will execute this operation atomically, i.e. without interference from any other operation and in order to maintain sequential consistency.

CORBA and Java

In Section 3.1.4 we discussed how logical memory sharing has been given a significant boost by the Object Request Broker architecture and the Java software tools. It is evident that these software technologies will enjoy heavy usage in distributed shared memory systems. A key concern will be the level of performance that DSM systems employing this technology will be able to obtain. Critical to the performance issue would be the handling of replication of objects and the management of consistency.

6.2 Transactions

In Chapter 5 we looked in some detail at several issues regarding the accessing of distributed resources. All of those issues are pertinent to this section. We all have some notion of a 'transaction'. It involves procedures undertaken to obtain some service or acquire some commodity. Indeed it is a mechanism for accessing resources. Within the areas of computer systems analysis, design, implementation and management one has to be pretty clear about the meaning of terms. For many entities there have to be exact definitions. This is no less true for a 'transaction'.

A user may request that some single operation be performed on a file, e.g. *open file-x*, or *read file-y*, etc. However, the user may like to perform a sequence of operations as in Figure 6.7.

In this sequence, there are multiple accesses forming a composite set of operations on the same file. During the processing of these operations it will be necessary to prevent access by any other user in order to avoid corruption of the stored information. Therefore we must regard both the single operation and the composite sequence in a certain sense as a single unit. This unit will be called a transaction. In order to identify transactions they must have explicit *begin* and *end* statements. Hence the sequence above could be expressed as in Figure 6.8.

```
open file-x
read file-x
write file-x
close file-x
```

Figure 6.7 A sequence of operations.

```
begin transaction
  open file-x
  read file-x
  write file-x
  close file-x
end transaction
```

Figure 6.8 A sequence of operations as a single transaction.

6.2.1 Concurrent transactions

Concurrency control techniques have to be implemented in order to serialize the transactions wherever problems can arise. Let Ri represent a read by transaction i and Wi represent a write by transaction i. Then concurrent processing of the two transactions 1 and 2 each with read and write operations can take, among others, the following sequences:

(a) R1W1R2W2
(b) R1R2W1W2
(c) R1R2W2W1.

Sequence (a) is safe, but (b) and (c) are not. For example, let transaction 1 represent a deposit of $100 to A's account while 2 represents a withdrawal of $100. With an initial sum of $300 in A's account, sequence (a) would leave the account showing $300, sequence (b) would leave the account showing $200, while sequence (c) would leave $400. Only sequence (a) did a correct update.

The update W1 in sequence (b) and the update W2 in sequence (c) are lost. This is an example of what is referred to as the *lost update* problem in concurrent transactions. Sequence (a) possesses a *serial* quality which has been shown always to generate correct results, i.e. each Ri must be immediately followed by its Wi.

Other problems associated with concurrent updates are the *uncommitted dependency* problem and the *inconsistent analysis* problem.

The uncommitted dependency problem arises when a transaction is allowed to access a data area that has been changed by another transaction but the change has not yet been committed. Since the update has not yet been committed, the possibility exists that it never will. Therefore, the first transaction could in fact have operated on data that 'never' existed.

The inconsistent analysis problem arises when a transaction performs some analysis based on an inconsistent state of the data. For example, let transaction S compute the present sum of two loan accounts, A and B, and let transaction T add $20 to A. A has value $100 and B has value $90. Assume the sequence of operations shown in Figure 6.9. The committed transaction, T, generated an inconsistent state for the transaction, S. The result obtained by S is inconsistent with the data stored.

S reads **A**
S assigns to sum the value of **A**, i.e. $100
T reads **A**
T adds $20 to **A** (i.e. A is now $120)
T commits
S reads **B**
S adds **B** to sum (i.e. sum is $190)

Figure 6.9 A sequence of operations on accounts A and B.

When the serial condition is not satisfied, these problems can arise. This safe property of serial processing has been extended and expressed in a formal theory of concurrency called **serializability theory** which formulates a precise condition for the correctness of concurrent transactions (Bernstein *et al.*, 1987).

Locking of the areas accessed has proven to be an adequate measure. However, there are always questions relating to the length of time that locks are held and the extent of the data areas that are locked. In addition, there is the problem of **deadlock** that can arise when resources can be locked away (see Section 5.2 on 'Concurrency').

The **two-phase lock** protocol has been adopted in many instances to control concurrent transactions. A transaction must acquire locks on the data areas to be accessed in the first phase (see Section 5.2). In the second phase, the locks are released. Having released a lock, a transaction cannot obtain a lock on the same or any other data item. Provision must be made to prevent, avoid or detect deadlocks. This may involve having to break locks and abort transactions in order to put the system back into production.

Name and password authentication at begin-transaction time can be done to ensure only authorized access. Access control lists will have to be maintained in order to perform the necessary checking. Capability-based techniques may also be employed to control access. These issues are discussed in Sections 4.1 and 4.2 under 'Naming and addressing' and 'Sharing'.

6.2.2 Atomic transactions

Software and hardware failures are a serious threat to the integrity of information systems (see Section 5.4). What is the state of a file in the event of such a failure during a file update? This problem is more severe when concurrent access to large databases is allowed. Some steps that can be taken involve making copies of critical material on separate physical volumes, and separating directory or indexing information from actual data.

An additional technique is the use of **atomic transactions**. An atomic transaction either completes successfully or has no effect. Any transaction which includes a change (an update) to any data item must be so handled that, should it

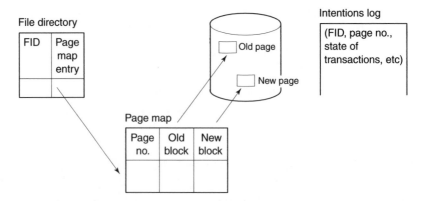

Figure 6.10 Atomic transaction using shadow-page technique.

not complete successfully, the change must be undone. Hence the system must maintain recoverable files.

The aim is to avoid overwriting the actual data in secondary storage. The use of a **shadow-page** technique is common among designers. We can assume that the data on the secondary storage medium are organized as files. Before updating a page of a file (or database), a free disk block/sector is obtained from the block allocation map. This block will be used to store the updated page. The page map of the file is appropriately modified to point to this new page in addition to maintaining the pointer to the old page. Furthermore, an **intentions log** may be used to record all these steps (see Figure 6.10).

A transaction has reached its **commit point** (or it can be committed) when any subsequent crash will not prevent the transaction from completing successfully. The commit point is, therefore, the point at which all changes to the data can be made permanent.

With the shadow-page technique, the transaction is committed when the new pages are completely updated, and the relevant entries have been made in the intentions log. During the update, the page exists in two versions: the shadow-page and the new page. When it is safe to make the change permanent, the file map is atomically updated to point to the updated page only. The space occupied by the shadow is therefore freed.

An alternative technique for recoverable files is the use of an **undo/redo log**. This technique involves appending a log record to a **log file** and making an entry in a log file map (see Figure 6.11). The log record may contain transaction ID, the pair (FileID, page number) of the page being updated, and the actual data contents of the page. The entry in the log file map associates the pair (FileID, page number) with the appropriate record in the log file.

Brown *et al.* (1985) have given five advantages that the log mechanism has over the shadow-page technique. These are as follows:

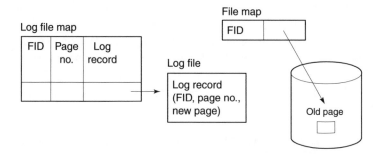

Figure 6.11 Atomic transaction using log technique.

1 The total cost of I/Os performed in the log technique is often less than that when using shadow-pages. The excess cost arises in the shadow-page technique because:

(a) it has to update the file map and the free block/sector allocation map recoverably;

(b) every read and write in the shadow-page technique is random, while the log technique does sequential writing and buffered reading which is less costly; and

(c) every transaction in the shadow-page technique requires an update of the file map, while the log updates the map only when the number of pages is altered. Since the pages updated by a transaction are not always clustered into one page of the file map, the file map update can be very costly.

2 The log technique supports sequential file organization on the disk where logically sequential pages are stored in a physically sequential manner. This improves the performance for sequential processing as well as random accesses. Random access is improved because the file map for the physically sequential file is smaller than for the non-sequential. The file map entries in the sequential case can point to longer physical extents. In the non-sequential file it is necessary to enter individual page addresses. Hence the shadow-page is more costly.

3 The logging technique can defer more work until after commit than the shadow-page. Whereas the shadow-page involves a write to the file pages before commit, the log does this after commit, hence responses in the log technique can be quicker. Furthermore, the implementation of the logging system may accommodate a stream of updates to the same file page before forcing the write to the appropriate disk sector.

4 File back-up is easier to implement in the log-based system. This involves two-copy logging and periodic file system dumps. With the shadow-page technique it may be necessary to introduce a logging system to provide back-up.

5 The logging system can be superimposed on an existing file system. There is no requirement for any special features in the implementation, since the log technique involves merely reading and writing files. Hence the implementation is less involved than for the shadow-page system.

We can therefore identify four key properties that transactions should have. These properties are:

1 Atomic: they are indivisible; they either succeed and commit or fail and leave no effect.
2 Consistent: they leave the system in a consistent state.
3 Isolated: they are serializable; concurrent transactions do not interfere with each other.
4 Durable: the changes made by committed transactions are permanent.

This is often called the ACID test of a transaction.

6.2.3 Two-phase commit

When a number of replicas are involved in the transaction the atomic condition can be satisfied by applying the **two-phase commit** protocol (Gray, 1978). The two-phase commit protocol requires a coordinator to maintain a record of the state of the transaction. In the first phase the coordinator sends a 'go either way' or 'prepare' message to all the participating sites. On receipt of this message, each site fulfils its local requirements for the support of atomic transactions.

When each site has succeeded in doing this it responds with a 'ready' or 'OK' message to the coordinator, otherwise its response will be 'abort' or 'not OK'. If all the responses received by the coordinator are positive, the coordinator will atomically change the state of the transaction to commit and begin the second phase by issuing a 'commit' message to the cooperating sites.

If there was a 'not OK' response in the first phase, or there was no response before some time-out, the coordinator will inform the sites to roll back. The coordinator waits until it has received responses to its second-phase messages from all the sites before the transaction is considered complete. Any failure during the whole exercise generates a restart procedure based on the state of the transaction as maintained in the coordinator's log.

6.2.4 Nested transactions

Often a transaction may require access to more than one resource. For example, it is customary for a banking transaction to transfer funds from one account to some other account. In a distributed system the separate resources that are to be accessed may be located at different sites. For situations like these it is useful to

```
begin transaction
  read file0-at-site0
  write file0-at-site0
  read file1-at-site1
  write file1-at-site1
  read file2-at-site2
  write file2-at-site2
end transaction
```

Figure 6.12 A multi-file, multi-site transaction.

have a transaction structure which affords some flexibility in how the collection of accesses and operations are managed.

For example, the transaction in Figure 6.12 can represent several different application contexts. What is clear is that three different files are being accessed and each file is at a separate site. It is quite possible that the accesses to these files can be done in parallel without causing any problems in the system. For example, it might represent the addition of an annual interest to three bank accounts held at different branches.

The nested transaction structure allows a transaction to create sub-transactions in a parent–child relationship. For example, Figure 6.12 can be expressed with nested transactions as in Figure 6.13.

All the children of a given parent transaction can run concurrently. The parent transaction can decide whether to commit or abort on knowing the outcome of the children. Each child can commit or abort independently of its siblings. However, the changes made by a committed child transaction are permanent only if its parent also commits. If the parent decides to abort, all the effects produced by its children, whether they had committed or not, are undone.

```
begin parent-transaction

begin child-transaction0
  read file0-at-site0
  write file0-at-site0
end child-transaction0

begin child-transaction1
  read file1-at-site1
  write file1-at-site1
end child-transaction1

begin child-transaction2
  read file2-at-site2
  write file2-at-site2
end child-transaction2

end parent-transaction
```

Figure 6.13 Nested transactions.

6.3 Summary

Distributed shared memory (DSM) and transactions are key issues in managing and accessing distributed resources. DSM allows programmers to use memory that is distributed over different computers as if it is a single shared memory. Transactions facilitate concurrent access to distributed resources (like distributed databases) without invalidating data integrity conditions.

DSM permits the sharing of either physical blocks of memory or logical data structures. The physical blocks are called pages, and page-based DSM is closely related to paged virtual memory systems. Logical structures shared in DSM include variables, procedures, objects and tuples.

The accesses to resources in a DSM system must be carefully controlled so as to achieve the agreed level of consistency. Either the consistency procedures may be transparent to the programmers, or the programmer may be required to use synchronization operations to indicate to DSM where mutually exclusive access is required.

Transactions must be atomic, consistent, isolated and durable. When these conditions are met the integrity of the resources is preserved. In a distributed system where resources are replicated and where network traffic and other conditions can fluctuate, specific transaction protocols must be adopted.

The two-phase commit protocol allows a coordinator to manage transaction commitment among a number of replicas across the network. Nested transactions facilitate increased parallel processing of transactions by letting a transaction generate child transactions. Siblings can run in parallel but the outcome of the transaction is determined by the parent transaction.

6.4 Questions

1   What is a distributed shared memory (DSM) system?
2   What forms can the shareable units in DSM take?
3   Distinguish between sequential consistency and release consistency in memory operations.
4   What is the function of the Page Manager in page-based DSM?
5   What is false sharing in DSM?
6   What advantage does sharing of logical structures have over sharing of physical blocks?
7   What is a transaction?
8   What is the ACID test of transactions?
9   Explain the following transaction processing problems: (a) lost update, (b) uncommitted dependency, and (c) inconsistent analysis.
10 Distinguish between the techniques of shadow-paging and undo/redo logs as used in atomic transaction processing.
11 What is a nested transaction?

12 What happens to the changes made by a committed child transaction in a nested transaction if the parent transaction aborts?

13 Refer to the Student Registration system in Question 23 of Chapter 5. Do you see DSM playing any significant role in this system? Do you see the Student Registration system supporting transactions? Why? If the system were to support transactions, give some examples of these transactions.

CHAPTER 7

Case studies

We shall study some implementations of distributed systems. There are many to choose from but we shall highlight a few that you are very likely to be using at present, or will use or hear much about in the future. We shall present distributed file systems, distributed databases, distributed operating systems and Internet-driven systems.

7.1 Distributed file systems

A distributed file system is a distributed system with the specific objective of providing network-wide file service (see Section 2.1). File service includes permanent storage of files and the controlled retrieval of information stored in those files. Users of the file system should be able to create, read, write and delete files. They should be provided with certain guarantees regarding privacy, security and performance, and enjoy the right to share their files with other users. In this section we shall discuss the *Network File System* and the *Andrew File System*.

7.1.1 Network File System (NFS)

NFS is a very popular client–server system designed by Sun Microsystems (Coulouris *et al.*, 1994; Tanenbaum, 1995). NFS allows an arbitrary number of clients and servers to share a common file system over local area or wide area networks. Every machine in NFS can be both a client and a server at the same time.

The server maintains a hierarchical directory system which can be accessed by remote clients in the system. The part of the server's directory system which clients can access (i.e. the list of directories) is classified as 'exported'. Clients access the server's system by mounting the exported directories (see Figure 2.6). When a directory is mounted so too are all its subdirectories and of course the files to which they point.

This mounting facility allows clients to maintain their own local filing system with appropriate intersections with a global filing system. Furthermore, a diskless workstation can mount the server's directories on its root directory. The workstation's filing system is then supported entirely on a remote server.

NFS also supports *automounting*. This feature allows a client to associate its local directory with a set of remote directories from which anyone can be selected as the target for a mount when a remote file is accessed. The client tries the set of servers that own the directories in parallel and selects the first one that responds. This affords some degree of fault-tolerance. Furthermore, through automounting users can implement replicated files by arranging that all the file systems specified in the automount are identical. NFS does not support replication directly.

Two or more clients can mount the same directory at the same time. Files can thus be shared in this way. It is up to the clients to coordinate the sharing. NFS merely ensures that only authentic clients are allowed access to the files. This can be done by associating clients with secret keys in a public key cryptographic system (see Section 4.5).

NFS does not support 'open' and 'close' file operations. Therefore the server does not have to maintain any information about open connections in between accesses to it. Consequently, should a server crash, no information about open files is lost. A server such as this, which does not maintain state information on open files, is referred to as **stateless**.

Clients can cache files in order to improve performance. However, this raises the cache coherence problem (see Section 4.3). NFS associates each cache block with a timer. When the timer expires the cache entry is discarded. Whenever a client opens a file that is already in its local cache a message is sent to the server to find out when the file was last modified. If the cached copy is not up-to-date it is discarded and a new copy is obtained from the server. Modified cache entries are written back to the server whenever the cache block timer expires.

7.1.2 Andrew File System (AFS)

AFS is a distributed file system developed at Carnegie-Mellon University to provide an information-sharing facility for thousands of workstations (Coulouris *et al.*, 1994). AFS is now marketed and maintained by Transarc Corporation. AFS, which is compatible with NFS, allows clients to access remote files via normal UNIX primitives. Its most important design goal was scalability.

Caching of whole files is key to this. When a client opens a file the whole file, if not already cached, is shipped to the client's cache. The cache survives reboots of the client's computer. Whenever possible, cached copies of files are used to satisfy client requests. When a client process closes a file, if the cached copy was updated, the server updates its copy. The cached copy is, however, retained to facilitate further requests at the same workstation.

The workstation cache is large enough to accommodate several hundred average-sized files. Therefore once a working set of currently and frequently used

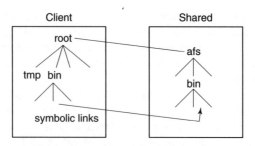

Figure 7.1 Shared files in AFS are accessible from a sub-tree
of the client's directory.

files are cached there is little or no traffic between client and server. If cache space is needed to accommodate a new download from the server, least recently used files are removed from the cache.

Clients can share files in AFS, i.e. the same file can be copied to separate workstation caches and accessed by concurrent processes. If any client updates its copy this is captured by the server only when the client closes the file. Indeed only the last update will be recorded at the server. When the server records an update to a file, all the clients holding cached copies are informed that their copies are now invalid and should be cancelled. Any further level of concurrency control must be handled independently among the client processes.

Files managed by AFS servers are classified as shared and are identified by a globally unique FID. Corresponding to this FID is a pathname which is used by the client in accessing the file. The pathname includes the root, a cell name, a volume and the filename, e.g. */afs/$AFSCELL/volume/filename*.

An AFS cell is a group of servers under a single administration typically using the same Internet domain name. A volume is a collection of files with a unique volume ID independent of the storage disks. Volumes containing frequently accessed data can be replicated for read-only access on several servers.

Shared files in AFS accessible from a given client form a sub-tree of the file directory at that client machine. This directory is a conventional UNIX file directory whose root points to both the AFS files and *local* files (see Figure 7.1). *Local* files are for the exclusive use of that client. AFS uses Kerberos to authenticate users (see Section 4.5).

7.1.3 Discussion

The distributed file system must possess some acceptable structure. NFS and AFS have adopted the client–server model. In NFS the server maintains a file directory, parts of which are 'exported'. These exported parts can be mounted by the clients. The mounted elements then form part of the clients' directories. AFS maintains a global directory of shared files. Pathnames are used by clients to access these files.

NFS and AFS allow the entire file to be shipped as the unit of access. This is facilitated by maintaining cached copies of files at client machines. The cache coherence issue is addressed differently. NFS uses timers while AFS invalidates cached copies when a client closes a file after an update.

AFS is designed to scale well. This is facilitated by its cache management. Both systems provide some security and concurrent access to the same file. Some replication is supported in AFS.

7.2 Distributed database systems

A distributed database system is a distributed system conforming to any of the design architectures outlined in Chapter 3, with the key objective of providing uniform access to cooperating databases possibly located at separate sites in a computer network. The important issues in distributed database design were discussed in Section 2.2. In this section we shall examine two example systems: *Oracle* and *Sybase SQL Server* (Bontempo and Saracco, 1995).

7.2.1 Oracle

Oracle, designed by Oracle Corporation, is a series of upward-compatible relational database systems. The latest releases possess distributed and gateway capabilities, and from Oracle 8 object types as well as relations are supported. The gateway facilities provide programmable and transparent access to non-Oracle database systems, file systems and a range of other applications. Oracle supports several network protocols including TCP/IP, DECnet and SNA. It is fully portable to scores of distinct hardware and operating system platforms, ranging from desktops through mainframes to supercomputers.

Oracle has a multi-threaded server architecture which increases the number of client connections that can be supported (see Sections 2.5, 3.1.3 and 4.3). A cost-based optimizer is used to improve the performance of query processing. The optimizer uses statistics like table (relation) sizes and location to find the most efficient access paths.

Oracle, through its Oracle Parallel Server, supports parallel transaction processing in shared disk environments. In this mode the Oracle servers can run in parallel on different processors in a multiprocessor configuration. Hence multiple separate transactions can be processed in parallel.

Concurrency control is handled by various locking mechanisms. Multiple update transactions can change a relation concurrently. This is possible since concurrency control locks can be applied on individual tuples of relations. Therefore, waiting is enforced only when there is an attempt to update the same tuple. Oracle can lock data at the tuple or relation level.

Oracle supports a multi-version consistency model also called a *non-blocking query technique*. In this model multiple versions of data are maintained and read operations do not block write operations. Transactions enjoy either statement-level read consistency or transaction-level read consistency. In statement-level read consistency a query sees only the latest version of data that existed when the query began. In transaction-level read consistency all the queries within a transaction see the same version of data.

Transaction processing enjoys complete location transparency. Atomic transactions are supported by a log-based technique with two-phase commit being used for applying updates (see Section 6.2). There is the facility for automatic asynchronous replication of relations. These replicas are read-only copies which can be refreshed at user-defined intervals.

7.2.2 Sybase SQL Server

Sybase, Inc. was one of the pioneers of 'client–server' relational database systems in their design of Sybase SQL Server in 1987. Sybase SQL Server is a family of client–server data access, storage and management products designed to meet the needs of large mission-critical database applications.

SQL Server controls concurrent transactions through locking mechanisms. Locks can be applied at page or table (relation) level. Read locks can be shared to allow multiple concurrent reads. Exclusive locks can be obtained to facilitate write transactions. Page-level locks are used as much as possible to improve the level of concurrency. Distribution and data storage statistics are used to optimize on the access paths in transaction processing.

SQL Server uses its Replication Server to support multiple copies of data. The replicas exist in a primary site/secondary sites arrangement. Any transactions committed to the primary site are automatically propagated to the secondary sites. If a failure prevents this automatic transfer from the primary to a secondary site, the primary site will store the information for a later retry. Any of the replicas can accept an update request. However, if a secondary site receives such a request, the request is redirected to the primary who does the update and then informs the secondary site to do likewise.

SQL Server handles updates which involve several databases. It uses a variant of two-phase commit to support atomic transactions. In standard two-phase commit all participating sites must be on-line to complete the transaction. However, Replication Server can store a transaction on behalf of an off-line site, and forward it later when the site becomes on-stream. Nested transactions are also supported (see Section 6.2).

SQL Server can operate on a wide range of platforms including PCs, Macs, UNIX workstations and Windows NT-based servers, as well as high-performance symmetrical multiprocessing systems. On multiprocessor systems multiple SQL Servers can be running in parallel, communicating with one another via shared memory. Through its OmniSQL Gateway, SQL Server allows read and write access to several relatively popular database management systems.

7.2.3 Discussion

The features provided by these two distributed systems are similar. The adoption of one system or the other is largely a marketing issue which addresses factors often unrelated to intricate technical design.

The basic database model used is the relation. Several types of locks are used to support concurrent transactions. Atomic transaction processing is supported through two-phase commit. Relations can be replicated in both systems. Each of these systems can run on multiple platforms including parallel execution on multiprocessor machines. Gateway facilities exist to several different popular database systems.

7.3 Distributed operating systems

The design of distributed operating systems was discussed in Section 2.5. The distributed operating system is a single network-wide operating system with its kernel and other key modules replicated at all the hosts/stations in the network. This allows uniform management of the hardware and software resources, and presents a single interface to the users irrespective of which network station is used. The examples we shall look at are *Amoeba*, *Chorus*, *Mach* and *Windows NT*.

7.3.1 Amoeba

Amoeba, developed at the Free University and the Centre for Mathematics and Computer Science in Amsterdam, has been described as one of the fastest distributed operating systems that have been reported. It offers high availability, parallelism, scalability and high performance while employing simplicity in design (Tanenbaum, 1995). In addition, Amoeba has a UNIX emulation package to increase the utility of the system.

Amoeba is an object-oriented system incorporating the client–server model. The facilities or resources in the network – hardware and software – are classified as 'services' and each service is managed by one or more server processes. Services can be public such as disk service, file service, database service, etc. Such services are considered to be long-lived in that they are operable for most if not all of the time. There are also short-lived private services which are created to meet specific program needs.

The client and server processes run in user space on top of a microkernel. The microkernel manages processes and threads, provides low-level memory management, supports communication, and handles low-level I/O. Threads allow multiple lines of execution within a process (see Sections 2.5, 3.1.3 and 4.3). The microkernel runs on all the machines in the system.

A server provides service by performing operations on objects, i.e. the service is implemented as the management of objects. A service is accessed through one or more ports. The object, upon which the server operates to provide the service, is identified and protected by a capability. The capability has the identity of the service port encoded into it.

Amoeba uses the remote procedure call (RPC) communication mechanism. There are three basic system calls to facilitate client–server interactions. Clients use the 'trans' to get service from a server; servers use the 'get-request' to announce their willingness to accept messages addressed to a particular port; and servers use the 'send-reply' to reply to the client. To receive service a message must be sent to one of the ports of the server.

Amoeba also supports group communication in which a message can be sent from a client to a group of processes. Processes can form a group to provide some service or carry out some task. A process can be a member of several groups at the same time. In order to obtain service provided by a group of processes, a client does an RPC with one of the members of the group. That member then uses group communication within the group to involve the other members in the exercise.

Processors in Amoeba belong to processor pools. A processor pool consists of many CPUs, each with its own local memory and network connection. This arrangement is to accommodate the trend towards installing increasing numbers of large multiprocessor systems. Processors are dynamically allocated from a pool to service user commands. Users do not need to know which processor or processors are allocated to their tasks.

One of the key contributors to Amoeba's good performance is its file system design. The file system runs as a collection of three servers: the *bullet server*, which handles file storage, the *directory server*, which handles file naming and directory management, and the *replication server*, which handles file replication.

The bullet server

This name is used to indicate the objective in the server design, that is, speed. A client uses a 'create' call to the server. The server returns a capability which can be used in subsequent accesses to the file. The user then gives the file an ASCII name which is then paired with the capability – (ASCII name, capability) – and given to the directory server.

The bullet server was designed to run on machines with large primary memory and a lot of disk space. Files, once created, cannot be changed; they are **immutable**. If there is need to change a file, a new file (with a different capability) must be created. The old one can be deleted or kept as a back-up.

Since a file cannot be altered after creation, its length is always known at creation time. Therefore, it can be stored contiguously on the disk and in the memory cache. This not only simplifies the storage management, but it allows a file to be read into memory in a single disk operation and hence it can be sent to the clients in a single RPC reply message.

It is expected that a client would create the entire file in its own main memory before sending it in a single RPC to the bullet server. However, if the client has

ASCII string	Capability set	Owner	Group	Other
notes	. . . .	1111	0000	1110
research	. . . .	1111	0010	1000
games	. . . .	1111	1100	0001
mail	. . . .	1111	1010	0100

Figure 7.2 Directory entries in Amoeba file system.

insufficient primary memory for the entire file, the *uncommitted file* option can be used. This allows a file to be 'in the process of creation'.

A client can append to an uncommitted file. At the end of creation the file is classified as *committed* at which time it takes on its immutable state. Uncommitted files cannot be read. The client with insufficient memory for an entire file cannot in that case benefit from the single RPC read of a file. That client is accommodated by allowing the reading of a section of a file. The client can therefore control the size of the transmitted portion.

The directory server

The primary function of the directory server is to provide a mapping from ASCII names to capabilities. Processes use the directory server to create, delete, update and look up directories. Directories are not immutable. They are objects which, like other objects, are protected by capabilities. Directory capabilities can be stored in other directories.

A directory entry is a row in a table (see Figure 7.2). The row pertains to the object (e.g. the file) that is included in the directory. The columns in the row indicate the ASCII name of the object, a set of capabilities each associated with a separate copy of the object stored at different bullet servers, and the access rights associated with different users.

The replication server

Objects managed by the directory server can be replicated automatically by using the replication server. The replication server operates in the background, scanning specified parts of the directory system periodically. On creation of an object, only one copy is made. The number of copies to be generated will be indicated in the directory. Whenever the replication server scans a directory and determines that more copies are to be made, it contacts the relevant servers for the additional copying to be done.

Amoeba is freely available over the Internet (*www.cs.vu.nl/pub/amoeba/*) for educational and research use.

7.3.2 Chorus

Chorus began as a research project in distributed operating system design at INRIA, France, in 1979. Its continued development was handled by Chorus Systems and in 1997 Chorus Systems was acquired by Sun Microsystems. Chorus contains a microkernel and a range of subsystems supported by that microkernel. Chorus enjoys relatively strong use in the embedded telecommunications and network infrastructure systems.

The microkernel, which provides minimal management of names, processes, threads, memory and communication, can be as small as 10 kbytes upon which dynamically loaded kernel processes can be run. These kernel processes support a layer of system processes to define a specific subsystem upon which user space processes can execute (see Figure 7.3). The kernel processes run in the kernel space while system processes run in user space.

The kernel process feature allows increased kernel functionality without permanently increasing kernel size. For example, different peripheral devices (disk I/O vs network interface) require different interrupt handlers. Therefore interrupt handlers are written as kernel processes and can be loaded dynamically when required by the hardware configuration. This ability to reconfigure Chorus is one of its strongest selling points.

The subsystems in Chorus provide UNIX emulation and other key services. Indeed, this subsystem architecture allows multiple operating system interfaces to exist on the same machine simultaneously. Key file systems like UNIX and NFS, and popular network protocols like TCP/IP, are supported.

The execution environment in Chorus is called an actor (or process) (Coulouris *et al.*, 1994). An actor can have one or more threads. Chorus has a message-passing system with ports. A port contains storage for a certain number of messages. A sender to a full port is suspended until sufficient space is available. Ports can be moved to other processes, even on other machines. Several ports can form a group to facilitate group communication. In addition to asynchronous

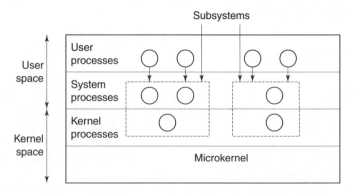

Figure 7.3 Chorus system structure.

message-passing using ports, Chorus also supports request–reply interactions (i.e. synchronous RPC communication) with ports.

7.3.3 Mach

Mach is a distributed operating system designed at Carnegie-Mellon University in the mid-1980s by a team headed by Richard Rashid (Black, 1990; Coulouris *et al.*, 1994). Mach is a message-passing system designed with UNIX compatibility, thus providing a comfortable environment for that large base of UNIX users.

UNIX is implemented in the user space where Mach can support other operating systems (see Figure 7.4). Mach therefore has a relatively small kernel (a microkernel) which is built as a base to support the operating system emulators. The system is designed to provide a distributed computing environment with flexible and transparent access to resources throughout the network. It manages both uniprocessor and multiprocessor nodes in a machine-independent manner.

Each host machine has the Mach microkernel which manages

(a) processes
(b) threads
(c) memory objects
(d) ports
(e) messages.

The process is the environment in which execution takes place, while the thread is an executable path through the process. Memory objects define the memory regions that can be allocated to a process as its address space. These objects form the basis of the Mach virtual memory system.

Mach uses the concept of a port for the transport of messages (see Section 5.1). Access to services and facilities provided by a process is through a port. Messages may be sent to and received from these ports which are controlled by the kernel (see Figure 5.3). A queue of messages can be formed at a port and each message

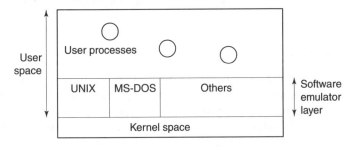

Figure 7.4 Layers in Mach.

will be handled or removed in turn. Mach supports both synchronous and asynchronous message passing. In the asynchronous mode, sender processes are not automatically blocked on sending messages.

The server process must first create a port through which the user processes can gain access to the service it provides. On port creation a capability name to that port and ownership of that port are given to the creator process. Before another process can remove a message from that port, it must be granted a receive capability to it. This receive access cannot be shared, but it can be passed to another process through a message. The initial owner of the port has receive access to it. Ownership can be passed to (but not shared with) another process.

On the creation of a process, it is allowed access to two ports for message passing to and from the kernel. One of these ports is called the 'kernel port' to which the created process has send rights, and the kernel has receive rights. Therefore the process can send messages to the kernel through this port. The other port is called the 'data port' to which the process has receive access and the kernel has send rights, hence the kernel can send messages to the process through this port.

The parent of a process can ask that its access rights to ports be given to the child process. Access rights to the 'kernel' and 'data' ports of the child process can also be given to the parent. In this way parent–child communication is supported by the same basic port mechanism.

Emergency messages are used to communicate errors and other matters which require immediate action. These messages have high priority and are therefore allowed to jump the queue at a port. One of the messages conveyed in this way is the notification of the destruction of a port to all processes that still have access to that port.

Communication across the network involves the 'network server' (see Figure 5.4). Messages destined for a remote host are sent to the port which belongs to the local 'network server'. This 'network server' sends the message to the 'network server' at the remote host. The remote 'network server' has the responsibility of sending the message to the port of the receiving process.

A very successful UNIX system that has been implemented on the Mach kernel is *OSF/1*. In addition to supporting distributed operation over the network, OSF/1 also supports symmetric multiprocessing computing nodes.

7.3.4 Windows NT

Microsoft's *Windows NT* through the *NT Server* supports the client–server model of distributed computing. This system is widely deployed, having benefited from the large market share enjoyed by the Windows operating system. Windows NT can support DOS, Windows, UNIX, OS/2 and Macintosh clients. It provides network management and administration, security and log-on control, and supports major networking and mainframe standards.

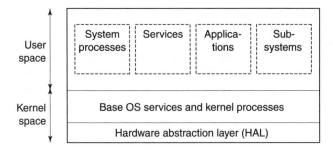

Figure 7.5 Windows NT system architecture.

Windows NT is designed to run on multiple hardware platforms, including uniprocessor and symmetric multiprocessor computers. The NT architecture comprises a number of layers (see Figure 7.5). These layers are, from the bottom up, the hardware abstraction layer (HAL), the kernel, the executive, and the subsystems. The HAL, kernel and executive run in kernel mode, while the subsystems share the user space with system processes, system services and user applications (see Solomon, 1998).

The HAL is a layer that isolates the rest of the operating system from the hardware and is therefore the basis for the system's portability. The kernel performs low-level OS functions like interrupt handling and thread scheduling. The executive handles the next level of OS functions like memory management, process and thread management, interprocess communication, security and so on. Although both the kernel and the executive run in kernel mode, the executive can be swapped in and out of memory, but the kernel cannot be swapped out.

Running in the user space are system and server processes, user applications and environment subsystems. The environment subsystems constitute a framework for the emulation of different operating systems. These operating systems use the native OS services provided by Windows NT and allow users to run programs in some preferred environment, e.g. OS/2.

High availability in distributed processing is provided by the Windows NT *Cluster Service* (Gamache *et al.*, 1998). The Windows NT cluster service allows a collection of computer nodes, called a cluster, to work together and appear to the users as a single large computer. The objective is to provide a system that is more reliable and powerful than a single node.

Clients in this cluster architecture interact with a *virtual Windows NT Server* that encapsulates the service and all the resources required to provide that service. The cluster service detects and restarts failed hardware and software components or, where possible, ships the functionality of a failed component to another node in the network.

The fundamental abstractions in the cluster service are *resource, resource dependencies* and *resource groups*:

- A *resource* is the basic unit of management in the cluster. A resource can be a hardware component such as a disk or software such as files.
- *Resource dependencies* are used to indicate when the availability of one resource depends on the availability of another resource.
- A *resource group* is a collection of resources that must be managed as a single unit. Operations performed on a group affect all the resources in that group, and if any resource in the group fails then the entire group is considered to have failed.

7.3.5 Discussion

Amoeba, Chorus and Mach are microkernel operating systems that allow other operating systems to run as subsystems above the microkernel. The primary system emulated is UNIX. Amoeba supports RPC and group communication, Chorus supports message passing and RPC, and Mach supports synchronous and asynchronous message passing.

Amoeba has a strong research and teaching thrust. Chorus is doing well in the embedded systems market and has the commercial backing of Sun Microsystems, while Mach was supported by the Open Software Foundation. Chorus has a reconfigurable kernel that can be adapted to different hardware configurations. Amoeba has a high performance file system facilitated by its immutable file feature.

Windows NT facilitates client–server interaction over the network. It supports other operating systems, and through its Hardware Abstraction Layer can be implemented on multiple hardware platforms. Through its Cluster Service, multiple server nodes can appear to the clients as a single machine. Windows NT enjoys a large installed base.

7.4 Internet-driven systems

The popularity of the Internet and the convenience of the World Wide Web have provided openings for innovative approaches to distributed system design. This has been so particularly in the area of client–server technology with client access through browsers to Web-based and other servers. Significant activities exist in the field of electronic commerce and the area of distributed object management with CORBA.

Electronic commerce, often called e-commerce, is viewed by many as buying and selling over the Internet. This is understandable since the Internet has created the opportunity to make one's business easily reachable from almost anywhere at any time. Other areas of e-commerce are in business-to-business exchanges over intranets or private networks. However, the dominant activity is in customer-to-business applications. A major player in this arena is *Viaweb*, now known as *Yahoo! Store*, which we shall examine in Section 7.4.1.

The object modelling approach to system design is enjoying increased use by computer practitioners. This trend has been due in no small measure to the availability of tools that allow the adoption of the object-oriented technologies. The CORBA technology facilitates the use, over the Internet, of objects managed by object request brokers (ORBs). The CORBA tool *Orbix* is being employed successfully in a number of distributed applications. We shall discuss two such applications in Section 7.4.2.

7.4.1 Yahoo! Store

Viaweb (now Yahoo! Store at *www.viaweb.com*) was started in 1995. Its chief architect, Paul Graham, described Viaweb's business as making 'software for making online stores' (Veitch, 1998). Users can make their own on-line stores and edit them through an ordinary browser. This customer-to-business type of e-commerce system is now an extremely active implementation area with hundreds of thousands of on-line stores envisaged in the foreseeable future.

All the software runs on the servers. The present servers are Pentium-based running a derivative of Berkeley UNIX. A server must keep track of its own state. The software is written in layers to facilitate modification and upgrade. There are four main components:

1   A WYSIWIG (What You See Is What You Get) editor that lets you edit your store through a browser. The editor is written in Common Lisp.
2   There is a C program to generate images.
3   An ordering system that is also written in C.
4   A program called the manager, written in Perl, through which merchants retrieve orders and analyse statistics.

Once the on-line store is set up, orders are accepted and can be retrieved securely using encryption to scramble credit card information. A merchant can view orders on the Web by clicking on the Manager button. Orders can also be retrieved as database files, or if the merchant has a server orders can be shipped to that server in real time.

On-line store items can be generated from a merchant's inventory files. A store can be updated as often as desirable from 'anywhere'. While a store is being updated visitors continue to see the previous version. Once the changes are committed the updated version becomes visible.

7.4.2 CORBA with Orbix

CORBA (see Section 3.1.4) is the Common Object Request Broker Architecture of the Object Management Group (OMG). CORBA facilitates distributed system implementation using reusable objects in client–server type interactions. The combination of CORBA technology and the Internet has increased the rate at which innovative distributed applications are being developed.

Orbix from IONA Technologies (*www.iona.com*) is at present the world's best-selling CORBA tool. The distributed applications designed using Orbix range from those with regional or local interest to those with an international market. In this section we shall look at a regional/Caribbean project and an international system implemented by American Airlines.

Road maintenance management with Orbix

A small team of researchers at the University of the West Indies – St Augustine designed and implemented a distributed system to facilitate road maintenance management in the Caribbean. CORBA technology was adopted and Orbix was used for system implementation (Mohan *et al.*, 1998a, 1998b).

The basic objective of the project was to keep track of the condition of roads, bridges and culverts in the region so as to manage effectively the maintenance of these facilities. In so doing there would be more efficient transport services which can impact positively on national development. Furthermore, although the entities in the system are primarily roads, the system is flexible enough to accommodate different application areas.

OrbixWeb, IONA Technologies' full implementation of the CORBA specification in the Java programming language, was used. This provides transparent access to the objects distributed across the network and, through Java, information can be accessed via the Internet by using a normal browser.

The system uses a three-level hierarchy of objects (see Figure 7.6). This captures the logical relation: roads and bridges within divisions, and divisions within country. Information to generate these objects, in a prototype system for Trinidad and Tobago, was obtained from the local Ministry of Works and Transport. These server objects are implemented in Java and made available to the distributed system through OrbixWeb.

Clients can access these objects through the Orbix-generated ORB. Servers can be registered at computers on the Internet. Clients use Java applets via a normal

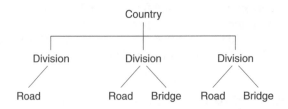

Figure 7.6 Hierarchy of objects.

browser to generate reports and other statistics on roads, bridges and culverts. At present the objects can be updated or created from Microsoft Excel files. Microsoft Excel was used since this software is familiar to the office staff of the Ministry of Works and Transport.

American Airlines on-line reservation

In the area of e-commerce over the Web, travel has emerged as the number one revenue generator, and the airline industry is in the forefront of this. American Airlines has refurbished its airline reservation system to capitalize on this Internet-enabled market (*Orbix Journal*, 1999).

Scalability and ease of use are two of the key features in the new system. The site captures and maintains enough information to provide personalized information to the user such as seating preference and desired ticket type. At the heart of this system is CORBA via Orbix.

The system is implemented as a number of layers (see Figure 7.7). At the top are the HTTP Server (with which the browser interacts) and an Interaction Manager. The next layer comprises dynamic objects (coded in C++) and the Travel Plan Data Store (which stores information specific to the users). The Orbix ORB is the third layer. In the fourth layer reside the SABRE reservation system and Oracle databases.

Through the ORB calls can be made transparently to servers on the same machine or across the network to remote machines. The ability to distribute the components of the system over several different machines helps address issues of load balancing and fault tolerance.

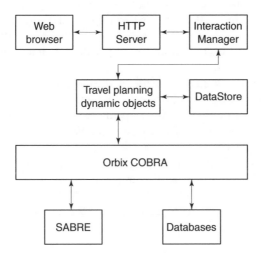

Figure 7.7 American Airlines Web-based reservation architecture.

7.4.3 Discussion

The Internet means ease of access to information or services at any time from anywhere. The browsers and the World Wide Web are key players in making the resources so easily accessible. The opportunity to engage in highly profitable business ventures over the Internet has been grasped with great excitement. E-commerce is becoming a dominant feature on the business landscape.

Object Request Broker architecture is being employed increasingly in the implementation of distributed systems. Orbix CORBA tools enjoy a significant share of this market. Systems from the small to the mission-critical enterprise-wide are adopting CORBA as the technology through which software can be reused and made available over the networks.

7.5 Summary

The case studies demonstrate that distributed system technology is working on many fronts. The study of these cases should help us appreciate how this technology is changing the way in which we conduct important parts of our everyday lives.

Distributed file systems make files available in a seamless manner across computer networks. The NFS and AFS are significant example systems. Client machines can cache copies of the files that they have accessed in order to reduce the communication with remote server machines. Mechanisms are available to address concurrency and consistency issues.

Distributed database systems facilitate access to cooperating databases over the network. Oracle and SQL Server are examples. These systems run on several different platforms and provide gateway access to other major database management systems. Parallel execution and multiple threads improve the transaction processing cycle.

Distributed operating systems provide all the normal operating system services and the additional services necessary to facilitate transparent use of the network. Microkernel architecture and multiple operating system emulation are some of the key features. Amoeba, Chorus, Mach and Windows NT have established marks in different places.

Distributed system design has been given a boost by Internet, browser and World Wide Web technologies. E-commerce is an area in which there is significant development. Common Object Request Broker Architecture is being used to reuse and tie software objects together for access across the networks. IONA's Orbix tools are enjoying major use in the implementation of CORBA systems.

7.6 Questions

1   What is 'mounting' in the Network File System (NFS)?

2   How does NFS handle cache coherence?

3   How does the Andrew File System (AFS) handle workstation caches?

4   How does AFS distinguish between local files and shared files?

5   What are some of the key technical features in (a) Oracle, (b) Sybase SQL Server?

6   What is an important consideration when choosing between these distributed database systems?

7   What are some of the key technical features in (a) Amoeba, (b) Chorus, (c) Mach and (d) Windows NT?

8   What are the important considerations when choosing from among distributed operating systems?

9   Identify some important Internet-driven distributed systems.

10   Identify the similarities and differences in the design of the on-line reservation and road maintenance systems discussed in this chapter.

Glossary

Abstract data type (ADT)   A data structure that has its implementation details hidden from the users.

Access method   The manner in which a communication channel is allocated to a computer which has information to transmit.

ACL   Access Control List. It lists the valid users of a resource.

Agent process   The process that serves as an interface between a local operating system and the computer network.

Amplitude modulation (AM)   A technique which employs changes in the amplitude of analog waves to represent digital signals.

Analog wave   A wave that has a continuous form. This differs from digital waves which are not continuous.

ARPA   Advanced Research Projects Agency of the US Department of Defense; now known as DARPA.

ARPANET   A pioneering network built by DARPA. ARPANET has grown into the Internet.

ATM (Asynchronous Transfer Mode)   Network technology which uses ultra-fast hardware switches to transmit fixed length data cells through the network.

Atomic broadcast   A message is delivered to all live members in a group or no one gets the message.

Atomic transaction   A transaction that either succeeds or has no effect.

Available copies (AC) protocol   A protocol used in replica management to allow read access to any copy and write access to all available copies.

Bandwidth   The range of frequencies that a channel can accommodate.

Baud rate   The number of times the signal changes in one second.

Bit stuffing   A system of adding redundant bits to a bit stream to preserve the uniqueness of some code.

Broadcast   A transmission technique where a message can be sent to all the members of a group at the same time.

Cable modem   Modulation device that modulates onto cable TV cable network. See modem.

Cache   Fast access primary store dedicated to a processor for the storage of frequently accessed data.

Cache coherence/consistency   The caches at the separate processors in a distributed system must be kept mutually consistent.

Capability   A name administered by the system and allocated to users for controlled access to objects. The user must supply this name in all attempts to access the associated object.

CCITT   An international organization that administers standards for telecommunications. CCITT is the abbreviation for Comité Consultatif Internationale de Télégraphique et Téléphonique.

Centralized lock controller   A central node that handles all the locks in a distributed system.

Checksum   A data field, usually at the end of a block of data, that facilitates the detection of errors that are in the block.

Ciphertext   The coded information transmitted in a cryptographic system.

Circuit switching   A communication environment in which a complete end-to-end channel is allocated for the duration of a communication session.

Client   The software module that resides at user machines and serves as the interface with some server in the client–server distributed system.

Codec   Coder–decoder. A device which converts analog signals to digital form for transmission and reconverts from digital to analog at the receiver.

Commit   An indication that a change to a data area is to be made permanent.

Commit point   The point after which a change will be considered permanent.

Computer network   A system of computers linked in a communications network.

Context-switching   The working environment of a processor is changed to begin execution on another process.

CORBA   Common Object Request Broker Architecture. An architecture which allows distributed applications to use and reuse objects across networks.

CRC (cyclic redundancy code)   A checksum computed using a generator polynomial as divisor and a polynomial representation of the message as dividend.

Cryptography   A system for transmitting encoded information:

  Public key cryptography   A public key is used for encoding and a different key (the private key) is used for decoding.

  Secret key cryptography   The same key is used for encoding and decoding the message.

Datagram   A packet that belongs to a message and is transmitted independently of the other packets in that message.

DCE   Data communication equipment. The communication processor in X.25 terminology.

DCE   Distributed Computing Environment. A software platform produced by the Open Software Foundation upon which distributed applications can run.

Deadlock   A situation where two or more processes/transactions are waiting on resources that another has and cannot release.

Decryption   The recovery of plaintext from ciphertext using a key.

Demodulation   The conversion of the analog signal back to a digital form.

DES   A widely used secret key cryptographic system.

Digital signalling   The transmission system that maps the digital values onto discrete voltage levels.

Digital signature   Electronic signature for verifying the origin of an electronic document.

DNS   Domain Name System. The system used by the Internet to resolve names onto computer addresses.

Download   To load from a server machine to a client machine.

DSL   Digital Subscriber Line. Modulation of digital signal onto previously unused higher bandwidth on the telephone companies' copper wire.

DSM   Distributed shared memory. In this model the address space of a program is distributed in a transparent way across the memories of separate computers.

DTE   Data terminal equipment. The device that forms the interface between the user and the X.25 link, e.g. the host computer.

Election algorithm   An algorithm used to elect a new leader of a group.

Electronic funds transfer   The facility to undertake monetary transactions through a computer network.

Encryption   The system of transmitting or storing information in a coded form.

Entity   The word used in database technology to refer to data elements that can be measured.

Error-correcting code   A data field that provides enough information both to spot an error and to derive the correct form.

Error-detecting code   A data field that provides information to detect an error.

Fail-soft operation   An environment where failures are not catastrophic.

FDDI (Fiber Distributed Data Interface)   A high performance fiber-optic ring LAN.

FDM (Frequency Division Multiplexing)   A mechanism for dividing a wide bandwidth channel into many narrow bandwidth channels for simultaneous use.

Frame   A string of bits enclosed within a begin-frame and an end-frame indicator.

Frame check sequence (FCS)   The checksum field that is appended to a frame.

Frame level control (FLC)   The field that contains control information on the frame.

Frequency   The number of complete waveforms that are generated in a second.

Frequency shift keying (FSK)   A modulation technique that maps the digital values onto different frequencies.

FTP   File Transfer Protocol. A widely used computer-to-computer file copying protocol.

Full-duplex   Information can travel in both directions at the same time.

Gateway A communication processor that links two networks.

Generator polynomial The polynomial used as the modulo 2 divisor in the generation of the cyclic redundancy code.

Guarded region A synchronization structure which involves a shared data area that cannot be entered before some boolean variable is true.

Half-duplex Information can be transmitted in both directions but in only one direction at a time.

Hertz (Hz) See Frequency.

Hierarchical model A structure that embodies a layered system.

Horizontal partitioning A distribution of a relation in a database where the subsets are some of the tuples with all their attributes.

Host A computer in the network that runs the user applications.

HTML HyperText Markup Language. The language used to facilitate storage of document preparation, formatting and other commands within the document itself. HTML is used for storing WWW pages.

HTTP HyperText Transfer Protocol. The protocol used for the transfer of HTML pages.

IDEA International Data Encryption Algorithm. It uses a 128-bit secret key.

Idempotent The property where repetition always produces the same effect as the original.

IDL Interface Definition Language. A language in which a server can specify its services to clients.

IEEE Institute of Electrical and Electronics Engineers.

IIOP Internet Inter-ORB Protocol. IIOP uses TCP/IP to facilitate inter-operability.

Immutable This term is used to refer to a file which cannot be changed after its creation.

IMP (Interface Message Processor) This term can be applied to the communications node in a network.

Indefinite postponement The inability to seize a resource when it becomes available. Someone always seems to get there before you.

Indeterminacy The principle of not being able to prescribe any schedule.

Inheritance A term used in object-oriented programming to refer to the facility to specify new objects in terms of a previously specified object.

Intentions log A record of the individual phases in a transaction in order to determine subsequent action in maintaining a recoverable system.

IP See TCP/IP.

ISDN Integrated Services Digital Network. A network facility that can provide a wide range of services including voice, teletext, fax, computer communications, etc.

ISO International Standards Organization.

Kerberos   A security system that is based on the Needham–Schroeder secret key authentication protocol.

Kernel   The part of the operating system that handles the lower level process scheduling, etc. It is always resident in primary storage.

LAN   Local area network. This covers a relatively small area like a building or a campus.

Livelock   A situation where the computing power is inordinately consumed by interrupt processing.

Location transparency   The characteristic of being able to function without knowledge of where the resources used are located.

Lock   A software mechanism that can prevent access to a shared resource.

Log file   A register of activities maintained to facilitate auditing and recovery.

Mail server   A software system that belongs to the client–server model. It allows users on the client machines to exchange mail.

Majority consensus   An update mechanism in a distributed system where the majority decision on which update to execute is carried.

MAN   Metropolitan area network. A city-wide computer network.

Mask   To temporarily disable some functional device.

Mbone   Multicast Backbone. The Internet architecture for multimedia transmissions.

Mbps   Mega (1 million) bits per second.

MD5   A message digest function used heavily on the Internet.

Message digest   A unique transformation of a message.

Message passing   An interprocess communication scheme that incorporates explicit send and receive functions.

Message switching   A transmission scheme which allocates the communication path in segments. At no time is a complete end-to-end path dedicated.

MHz   Megahertz, million cycles per second. See Frequency.

MIME   Multipurpose Internet Mail Extensions. The protocol used on the Internet to accommodate a comprehensive range of types in mail documents.

Modem   Modulator/demodulator. A device used in the conversion of digital signals to analog form and vice versa.

Monitor   A synchronization data structure implemented in software to control the access to shared variables and procedures.

Mounting   A facility which allows clients to link their filing systems to that of the file server.

MPEG   Motion Picture Experts Group. Sets standards for audio and video storage, retrieval and transmission.

MPI   Message Passing Interface. A message passing standard which facilitates the programming of parallel and distributed applications.

Multicast   A message is sent to all members of a group.

Multiplexing The technique that allows the sharing of a single channel by several stations.

Multiplexor A device that implements multiplexing.

Name server A client–server system that provides resource naming and location services.

Network operating system A system of heterogeneous operating systems co-operating through agent processes in a computer network.

Network transparency The facility to use the services of a computer network without being aware that the network exists.

NNTP Network News Transport Protocol. The protocol used by the Internet to transport news items.

Node A processing unit that is linked into a communications network.

NTP Network Time Protocol. The Internet clock synchronization algorithm.

OMG Object Management Group. A consortium of computer vendor and end-user companies with the objective of creating a standard for interoperability across computer networks using object-oriented technologies.

Optical fibers Transmission media that convey light signals.

Optimistic scheme A transaction processing scheme that delays multi-site consistency checks until after the transaction is processed.

ORB Object Request Broker. See CORBA. The ORB manages the interactions between clients and server in CORBA.

OSF Open Software Foundation. A consortium of computer vendors producing UNIX and other related software standards.

OSI Open Systems Interconnection.

Packet A fixed length string of bits which is usually the smallest extent of information transmitted in the network.

Packet switching Messages are divided into fixed length packets and each packet is transmitted independently one hop at a time. An entire end-to-end path is not dedicated. See Message switching.

Packet Switching Node (PSN) The communications processor in a packet switching communications subnet.

Page A fixed number of bytes that can be individually addressed and manipulated.

Page map A data table that associates pages in a file with their location in storage.

Parallel Virtual Machine (PVM) The use of networked workstations to simulate a parallel computer.

Parameter marshalling The packing of parameters into a message for transmission to a remote site. The primary objective is the preservation of semantic integrity.

Partition failure A failure that causes some component of the distributed system to be cut off from the remainder.

Partitioning The division of a distributed database system into distinct parts for separate storage.

PEM Privacy Enhanced Mail. An official Internet security system for email.

Period The number of seconds taken by a wave to complete one cycle.

Periodic A wave that repeats its shape with time.

Pessimistic protocol A protocol in transaction processing that requires consistency checking before executing the transaction.

PGP Pretty Good Privacy. An easily available security system originally developed by Philip Zimmermann.

Phase change A difference in angular measure between waves of the same shape.

Phase modulation (PM) A modulation technique that represents the digital values by phase changes.

Plaintext Information that has not been coded.

Point-to-point network A network in which stations have direct links to other stations. There is no physical broadcast capability.

Polling A mechanism used to determine whether stations have information to transmit.

Polynomial code See CRC.

Port A mechanism used to receive inputs or messages. It can be viewed as an address at which messages can be delivered for the owner of the port.

Primary key The unique identifier of a record.

Primary node/site The node or site at which updates are performed immediately in a distributed system. All other copies are updated later.

Printer server A software system that belongs to the client–server model. It allows users on client machines access to a common printer.

Procedure call The facility to start execution of another procedure by naming that procedure. The caller waits until the called procedure completes and returns control.

Protocol The specifications which when followed make communication among similar objects possible.

PSN See Packet Switching Node.

Pulse code modulation (PCM) A technique used to convert analog signals to digital form. Eight bits are used to convey the information derived from every sample of the analog signal. This signal is sampled 8000 times per second.

PVM See Parallel Virtual Machine.

Query processing The handling of user requests that are made to the database system.

Quorum consensus A distributed transaction processing protocol that requires that a quorum of nodes agree on which transaction is to be processed.

RAID   Redundant Array of Inexpensive Disks. A data block is spread across a number of disks in order to facilitate faster response afforded by the parallel access to each disk.

Relation   A two-dimensional structure of entity occurrences and their attributes.

Relational model   A system that embodies the relation as the basic data structure.

Remote procedure call (RPC)   A procedure call mechanism that extends to remote sites. See Procedure call.

Repeater   A device that strengthens (repeats) a signal.

Replication   To hold a copy of a file/object at another site.

Roll-back   To undo the effect of a transaction.

Root directory   The global parent node in a tree-structured directory system.

Root of file   The page that contains the header and the page map of the file.

RSA   Rivest–Shamir–Adelman public key cryptographic system.

Semijoin   A variant of the join operator that is used to reduce the communication cost.

Serializability   The scheduling of transactions so that their execution will produce the same effect as if they were performed serially.

Server   The software module that manages a service and is located at the machine where the service resides.

Shadow-page   In order to implement recoverable files, the actual file page is not updated. A new block is allocated for the update during which time the page has two versions: the new one and the old or shadow.

Simplex   A mode of transmission that permits information flow in only one direction.

Single-shot protocol   Requests are repeatable and responses are not saved by the server.

SMTP   Simple Mail Transport Protocol. Widely used protocol to transmit email.

Socket   A software interface to TCP/IP.

Spatial locality   Processing activity is dispersed among neighbouring locations over some small interval of time.

SSL   Secure Sockets Layer. A security protocol that provides secure client/server communications over the Internet.

Stateless   Information on the state of an object is not maintained.

Station   A device that allows user access to the network.

STDM (Statistical Time Division Multiplexing)   A technique used to multiplex a channel among several stations. Time slots are allocated based on the expected user demand which allows more user stations than time slots.

Store-and-forward   Messages are routed through the network one IMP-to-IMP link at a time. See IMP (Interface Message Processor).

Stream   A name given to connection-oriented transmissions. A connection-oriented service preserves the order in which packets are transmitted.

Striping   Disk striping is used in RAID technology. In striping the data is stored across a number of disks.

Synchronization   The programming of different activities so that they operate in step with each other.

TCP/IP (Transmission Control Protocol/Internet Protocol)   Transport and network protocols used in the Internet.

TDM (Time Division Multiplexing)   The sharing of a single channel among several stations by allocating each station a time slot.

Telnet   A widely used protocol for remote login to computers on the Internet.

Temporal locality   Processing activity is concentrated repeatedly in the same location for some small interval of time.

Thread   A mini-process within a process facilitating concurrency at a level below the process.

Three-message protocol   A communication protocol that involves a request, response and acknowledgement sequence.

Transmission rate   The rate at which the digits are transmitted.

Transparency   The details of the system are hidden from the user.

Tree model   A software system that is structured like a tree. Child nodes have only one parent node.

Two-phase commit   A technique used in distributed systems to implement recoverable updates. All participating sites must be coordinated to ensure that all sites behave in the same manner. This involves two phases.

Two-phase lock (2PL)   A locking protocol used in distributed systems which involves a locking of all needed resources before beginning a transaction, and a release phase. Once a resource is released it cannot be reclaimed.

UDP   User Datagram Protocol. Connectionless transport protocol used in TCP/IP.

Undo/redo log   A log file that supports recoverable files. See Log file.

URL   Uniform Resource Locator. The format used for symbolic addressing over the Internet.

UTC   Universal Coordinated Time. The globally correct time provided via UTC shortwave radio or satellite services.

Vector timestamp   A timestamp which allows the number of updates originating from each member in a group to be recorded.

Vertical partitioning   The division of a relation into partitions such that a partition contains some of the attributes for all the tuples.

Virtual call/circuit   The same communication path is used for the delivery of all packets in a message and the sequence is maintained.

Virtual memory   A system which allows executable programs to be larger than the primary storage. Programs are divided into pages and held on secondary storage. Pages are mapped onto primary storage blocks at runtime.

VOD   Video On Demand. A system where a video server maintains videos which home users can access via a communication network.

Voting scheme   A distributed transaction processing scheme in which a required number of votes must be collected before processing can begin.

WAN   Wide area network.

WWW   World Wide Web. The dominant information resource and accessing capability on the Internet.

X.21, X.25   CCITT network access protocols that are incorporated in the ISO–OSI reference model at layers 1, 2 and 3.

X.500   A directory service defined by CCITT and ISO.

XML   eXtensible Markup Language. A markup language used for defining the types of documents handled by the WWW.

References

Arnold, K. and Gosling, J., 1996. *The Java Programming Language*, Reading, MA: Addison-Wesley.

Asokan, N., Janson, P.A., Steiner, M. and Waidner, M., 1997. The state of the art in electronic payment systems, *IEEE Computer*, **30**, 9 (Sept.), 28–35.

Bal, H.E., Bhoedjang, R., Hofman, R., Jacobs, C., Langendoen, K. and Ruhl, T., 1998. Performance evaluation of the Orca shared-object system, *ACM Transactions on Computer Systems*, **16**, 1 (Feb.), 1–40.

Ben-Ari, M., 1990. *Principles of Concurrent and Distributed Programming*, Englewood Cliffs, NJ: Prentice Hall.

Bernstein, P.A., Hadzilacos, V. and Goodman, N., 1987. *Concurrency Control and Recovery in Database Systems*, Reading, MA: Addison-Wesley.

Birman, K.P. and Joseph, T.A., 1987. Exploiting virtual synchrony in distributed systems, *ACM SIGOPS Operating Systems Review*, **21**, 5, 123–138.

Birrell, A.D. and Nelson, B.J., 1984. Implementing remote procedure calls, *ACM Transactions on Computer Systems*, **2**, 1 (Feb.), 39–59.

Black, D.L., 1990. Scheduling support for concurrency and parallelism in the Mach operating system, *IEEE Computer*, **23**, 5 (May), 35–43.

Bontempo, C.J. and Saracco, C.M., 1995. *Database Management, Principles and Products*, Englewood Cliffs, NJ: Prentice Hall.

Brinch Hansen, P., 1978. Distributed processes: a concurrent programming concept, *Communications of the ACM*, **21**, 11, 934–940.

Brown, M.R., Kolling, K.N. and Taft, E.A., 1985. The Alpine file system, *ACM Transactions on Computer Systems*, **3**, 4 (Nov.), 261–293.

Carriero, N. and Galernter, D., 1989. How to write parallel programs: a guide to the perplexed, *ACM Computing Surveys*, **21**, 3, 323–357.

Coulouris, G., Dollimore, J. and Kindberg, T., 1994. *Distributed Systems, Concepts and Design*, 2nd edition, Reading, MA: Addison-Wesley.

Crichlow, J.M., 1994. Combining optimism and pessimism to produce high availability in distributed transaction processing, *ACM SIGOPS Operating Systems Review*, **28**, 3 (July), 43–64.

Crichlow, J.M., 1997. *An Introduction to Distributed and Parallel Computing*, 2nd edition, Englewood Cliffs, NJ: Prentice Hall.

Crichlow, J.M., Mohan, P. and Devenish, R., 1997. Distributed concurrency control with objects, *Proceedings of the IASTED International Conference on Software Engineering*, 2–4 Nov., San Francisco, California, 307–310.

Date, C.J., 1995. *An Introduction to Database Systems*, 6th edition, Reading, MA: Addison-Wesley.

Davidson, S.B., Garcia-Molina, H. and Skeen, D., 1985. Consistency in partitioned networks, *ACM Computing Surveys*, **17**, 3 (Sept.), 341–370.

Deitel, H.M. and Deitel, P.J., 1994. *C: How to Program*, 2nd edition, Englewood Cliffs, NJ: Prentice Hall.

Deitel, H.M. and Deitel, P.J., 1997. *Java: How to Program*, Englewood Cliffs, NJ: Prentice Hall.

Dongarra, J.J., Otto, S.W., Snir, M. and Walker, D., 1996. A message passing standard for MPP and workstations, *Communications of the ACM*, **39**, 7 (July), 84–90.

Farrag, A.A. and Ozsu, M.T., 1989. Using semantic knowledge of transactions to increase concurrency, *ACM Transactions on Database Systems*, **14**, 4 (Dec.), 503–525.

Fayad, M.E. and Schmidt, D.C., 1997. Object-oriented application frameworks, *Communications of the ACM*, **40**, 10 (Oct.), 32–38.

Francis, M.F. and Crichlow, J.M., 1995. A mechanism for combining optimism and pessimism in distributed processing, *Proceedings of the IASTED/ISMM International Conference on Intelligent Information Management Systems*, Washington, DC (June), 103–106.

Freeman, T.L. and Phillips, C., 1992. *Parallel Numerical Algorithms*, Englewood Cliffs, NJ: Prentice Hall.

Gamache, R., Short, R. and Massa, M., 1998. Windows NT clustering service, *IEEE Computer*, **31**, 10 (Oct.), 55–62.

Geist, A., Beguelin, A., Dongarra, J., Jiang, W., Manchek, R. and Sunderam, V., 1994. *PVM: Parallel Virtual Machine, A Users' Guide and Tutorial for Networked Parallel Computing*, MIT Press.

Gifford, D.K., 1979. Weighted voting for replicated data, *Proceedings of the 7th ACM Symposium on Operating Systems Principles*, Dec., 150–162.

Goscinski, A., 1991. *Distributed Operating Systems, The Logical Design*, Reading, MA: Addison-Wesley.

Gray, J.N., 1978. Notes on database operating systems, *Lecture Notes in Computer Science*, **60**, 393–481, Springer-Verlag, Berlin.

Handley, M. and Crowcroft, J., 1995. *The World Wide Web, Beneath the Surf*, University College London, UCL Press Limited.

Hoare, C.A.R., 1978. Communicating sequential processes, *Communications of the ACM*, **21**, 8, 666–677.

Jajodia, S. and Mutchler, D., 1990. Dynamic voting algorithms for maintaining the consistency of a replicated database, *ACM Transactions on Database Systems*, **15**, 2 (June), 230–280.

Johnson, R.E., 1997. Frameworks = (components + patterns), *Communications of the ACM*, **40**, 10 (Oct.), 39–42.

Kalicharan, N., 1994. *C by Example*, Cambridge: Cambridge University Press.

Kernighan, B.W. and Ritchie, D.M., 1978. *The C Programming Language*, Englewood Cliffs, NJ: Prentice Hall.

Lamport, L., 1990. Concurrent reading and writing of clocks, *ACM Transactions on Computer Systems*, **8** (Nov.), 305–310.

Li, K. and Hudak, P., 1989. Memory coherence in shared virtual memory systems, *ACM Transactions on Computer Systems*, **7**, 4 (Nov.), 321–359.

Liskov, B. and Ladin, R., 1986. Highly available distributed services and fault-tolerant distributed garbage collection, *Proceedings of the Fifth Annual ACM Symposium on Principles of Distributed Computing*, Aug., 29–39.

Lynch, N.A., Blaustein, B.T. and Siegel, M., 1986. Correctness conditions for highly available replicated databases, *Proceedings of the Fifth Annual ACM Symposium on Principles of Distributed Computing*, Aug., 11–28.

Millikin, M.D., 1994. DCE: Building the distributed future, *Byte*, **19** (June), 125–134.

Mitchell, J.G., 1982. *File Servers for Local Area Networks*, Palo Alto, CA: Xerox PARC.

Mohan, F., Brereton, M. and Crichlow, J.M., 1998a. Building distributed computer systems for the Caribbean – the Roads Maintenance System example, *Proceedings of the 9th AGM of the Caribbean Academy of Sciences*, 28–30 May, Guadeloupe.

Mohan, F., Crichlow, J.M. and Mohan, P., 1998b. A road system that leads yesterday's investment into tomorrow's technology, *Proceedings of the IASTED International Conference on Software Engineering*, Las Vegas, 28–31 October, 99–102.

Naugle, M.G., 1991. *Local Area Networking*, New York: McGraw-Hill.

Needham, R.M. and Herbert, A.J., 1982. *The Cambridge Distributed Computing System*, Reading, MA: Addison-Wesley.

Orbix Journal, 1999. Sight & Sound Software, American Airlines, Iona Technologies, **Q1**, 32–34.

Orfali, R. and Harkey, D., 1998. *Client/Server Programming with JAVA and CORBA*, 2nd edition, New York: John Wiley & Sons.

Paris, J.-F. and Long, D.D.E., 1990. The performance of available copy protocols for the management of replicated data, *Performance Evaluation*, **11** (North-Holland), 9–30.

Powell, D., 1996. Group communication, *Communications of the ACM*, **39**, 4 (Apr.), 50–53.

Solomon, D.A., 1998. The Windows NT Kernel architecture, *IEEE Computer*, **31**, 10 (Oct.), 40–47.

Stallings, W., 1995. *Operating Systems*, 2nd edition, Englewood Cliffs, NJ: Prentice Hall.

Stenstrom, P., 1990. A survey of cache coherence schemes for multiprocessors, *IEEE Computer*, **23**, 6 (June), 12–24.

Stroustrup, B., 1991. *The C++ Programming Language*, 2nd edition, Reading, MA: Addison-Wesley.

Svobodova, L., 1984. File servers for network-based distributed systems, *ACM Computing Surveys*, **16**, 4, 353–398.

Tanenbaum, A.S., 1995. *Distributed Operating Systems*, Englewood Cliffs, NJ: Prentice Hall.

Tanenbaum, A.S., 1996. *Computer Networks*, 3rd edition, Englewood Cliffs, NJ: Prentice Hall.

Thomas, R.H., 1979. A majority consensus approach to concurrency control for multiple copy databases, *ACM Transactions on Database Systems*, **4**, 2 (June), 180–209.

Ullman, J.D., 1982. *Principles of Database Systems*, 2nd edition, Rockville, MD: Computer Science Press.

Veitch, J., 1998. A conversation with Paul Graham, *Communications of the ACM*, **41**, 5 (May), 52–54.

Walker, B., Popek, G., English, R., Kline, C. and Thiel, G., 1983. The LOCUS distributed operating system, *Proceedings of the Ninth ACM Symposium on Operating Systems Principles*, **17**, Bretton Woods, New Hampshire, 5, 49–70.

Wang, Y., Liu, J.C.I., Du, D.H.C. and Hsieh, J., 1997. Efficient video file allocation schemes for video-on-demand services, *Multimedia Systems*, **5**, 5, 283–296.

Wittie, L.D., 1991. Computer networks and distributed systems, *IEEE Computer*, **24**, 9, 67–76.

Index

abstract data type (ADT), 53
access control list (ACL), 15, 82, 98, 104, 139
actor, 154
Ada, 44–6
addressing, 77–81, 104
agent, 38
airline reservation, 11, 161
Amoeba, 151–53, 158, 162, 163
Andrew File System (AFS), 146, 147–9, 162, 163
ARPANET, 2, 60, 73
ATM, Asynchronous Transfer Mode, 74
AT&T, 53
atomic
  broadcast, 49
  transaction, 125, 139–42, 144, 150, 151
  update, 125, 128
authentication, 81, 98, 99, 100, 101, 103, 104, 105, 139
availability, 15, 22, 26, 28, 33, 48, 77, 84–91, 104, 119, 126, 127, 151, 157, 158
available copies (AC) protocol, 125, 128

bandwidth, 9, 64, 65, 66
baud, 61
Bell Laboratories, 53
Berkeley, 112, 122, 128, 159
bit stuffing, 68
bridge, 2, 85
broadcast, 49, 60, 70, 79, 111
bulletin board, 6, 7, 43, 74
bus, 85

C, 10, 47, 52, 55, 136, 159
C++, 10, 47, 53–4, 55, 56, 161
cable modem, 63, 64

cache, 21, 80, 86, 91, 105, 147, 148, 149, 152, 162
  coherence/consistency, 22, 86–7, 120, 147, 149, 163
capability, 15, 78, 82, 98, 139, 152, 153, 156
  list, 82, 104
Carnegie-Mellon University, 147, 155
CCITT, 81
Chorus, 151, 154–5, 158, 162, 163
client–server, 8, 21, 43, 50–2, 103, 106, 114, 124, 146, 148, 150, 151, 152, 156, 158
clock, 34, 49, 94, 96, 118, 121–3, 124, 127
Cluster Service, 157, 158
coaxial cable, 64
codec, 63
commit point, 140
communication
  bandwidth, 33, 34
  channel, 3, 29, 59, 60, 85, 88, 106, 112
  cost, 29, 83, 93
  inter-process, 40, 70, 71
  intra-process, 40
  link, 3, 9, 28, 66, 85, 125
  load, 29, 32, 34, 37
  medium, 3
  processor, 2
  protocol, 23, 34, 49, 85
  subnet, 2
  traffic, 27, 33, 34, 48, 91
components, 58–9, 84
computer vision, 10
concurrency, 16, 88, 106, 114–20, 150, 162
  control, 22, 83, 127, 138, 139, 148, 149
congestion, 70, 73, 85
connection-oriented, 69, 71, 73, 112, 113, 114